Praise for *There Is No Box*

"*There Is No Box* is a critically important book, offering invaluable insights and a clear path forward to becoming a relatable leader. Professor Cleveland's premise that leadership is more than a skill, it is a lifestyle, is exactly on point. And his conclusions are based on strategies drawn from real-world experience. As a former United States ambassador serving under President Ronald Reagan, I strongly concur with his observation that the power of cross-cultural competence is essential for becoming a successful leader."

—Paul A. Russo, United States Ambassador (ret.)

"Marisa and Simon in *There Is No Box* have captured the essence of leadership by bringing to light relatability as the primary driver to success, with communication and compassion as central elements. Their gifted approach to leadership is grounded in established theory and reinforced by continuous reflection exercises based on their vast experience in leading diverse teams of people. The road map to relatable leadership offers a synergistic right and left-brain perspective that will benefit anyone desiring a clear path to leadership success as presented through the lens of proven leaders."

—Paul Dooley, PhD, former Assistant Secretary General, United Nations

"*There Is No Box* challenges our leaders—emerging and established—to focus on the importance of finding common ground amid a landscape of global and digital diversification. The authors weave together a method for becoming a relatable leader and taking charge of your own life. This is the book that every leader should share with their teams so they can thrive intellectually and emotionally. Based on my experience as a lawyer, ethics professor, and policy maker, I'm impressed with the way the authors blend academic theory with real-world implementation."

—Paul Lewis, JD, former Special Envoy at the U.S. Department of Defense

"Today we live in a volatile, uncertain, complex, and ambiguous (VUCA) world. The complexities organizations face everyday cry out for effective and relatable leaders to successfully navigate change. This book provides a clear road map on how to become a relatable leader to drive change while fulfilling your destiny. As Marisa and Simon Cleveland point out: Leadership isn't a trait; leadership is a lifestyle.'"

—Timothy Mills, CSM PMP, Instructor, Agile Project Management, Harvard Extension School – Dept. of Continuing Education, Harvard University, Cambridge, MA

"*There Is No Box* is a sensible, skillfully assembled, eminently readable survey of the most important aspects of being a leader and a human being. The authors inspire you to think about leadership as a state of being that can be found throughout any level and sphere of life, not just in the workplace. Relatable leadership and cultural agility, the book's main contributions to leadership literature, have changed the way I lead and live my life. You might feel uncomfortable, but then you'll feel grateful to prioritize your own leadership development."

—George Moschoglou, PhD, Associate Professor of the Practice and Faculty Director, Georgetown University

"*There Is No Box* presents a fresh view of leadership through the lens of what the authors call 'relatable leadership.' The concept of relatable leadership builds on the findings of prior studies, which found that there is no one best style of leadership that fits all situations. However, developing a relatable style will help one adapt to present-day situations where diversity, equity, and inclusion are center stage. The authors go beyond discussing the topic by providing a framework for developing a relatable leadership style based on project management concepts. *There Is No Box* is a great read for those just starting out, those sensing that they need to change their approach to leadership, or even those who just want to look outside the existing leadership style boxes."

—Dr. Jack Deem, Academic Department Chair, School of Business and Information Technology, Purdue Global University

"*There Is No Box* shows us all the ways to step outside of our comfort zone, embrace ambiguity, and leverage our experiences of immovable boundaries and rigid playbooks to create a new paradigm between a leader and those they influence."

—Mary Ludden, MBA, PhD, Senior Vice Chancellor and Senior Vice Provost, Northeastern University

THERE IS
NO BOX

THERE IS
NO BOX

A Practical Guide
for the Relatable Leader

MARISA CLEVELAND
AND SIMON CLEVELAND

Matt Holt Books
An Imprint of BenBella Books, Inc.
Dallas, TX

Matt Holt is an imprint of BenBella Books, Inc.
10440 N. Central Expressway
Suite 800
Dallas, TX 75231
benbellabooks.com
Send feedback to feedback@benbellabooks.com

BenBella and *Matt Holt* are federally registered trademarks.

Printed in the United States of America
10 9 8 7 6 5 4 3 2 1

Library of Congress Control Number: 2022017975
ISBN 9781637741948 (hardcover)
ISBN 9781637741955 (electronic)

Editing by Katie Dickman
Copyediting by Ruth Strother
Proofreading by Isabelle Rubio and Madeline Grigg
Indexing by WordCo Indexing Services, Inc.
Text design and composition by PerfecType, Nashville, TN
Cover design by Brigid Pearson
Printed by Lake Book Manufacturing

Special discounts for bulk sales are available. Please contact bulkorders@benbellabooks.com.

For our moms, Joan and Ionka,
for teaching us that even though we might not fit in,
we shouldn't be afraid to stand out.

During childhood, we're told to color inside the lines. In our twenties, we're asked to think outside the box. But what if there is no box?

Leadership is not a trait; leadership is a lifestyle.

CONTENTS

FOREWORD

My career in leadership began in a much different world than we live in today. It was more common than not that those leaders of yesteryear would follow command and control approaches, or theory *x* type of leadership styles. What this meant is that they were "the boss" and you took your direction from them with little opportunity to discuss alternative solutions to emerging challenges. It was also quite common to work in an "us vs. them" environment with management on one side of an argument and employees on the other side with a fair amount of mistrust in the middle. You certainly wouldn't have categorized your boss as compassionate or culturally agile two decades ago. Phrases that were commonly injected into my daily meetings were "stay in your lane" or "that's not your role," which were used as levers of control by top management and meant to limit your influence on organizational outcomes. A multitude of environmental forces have now conspired to force leaders of today into confronting their own positionality and explore adopting contemporary approaches to inspiring teams in a way that few of us could have imagined even five years ago.

Even after all these years, I consider myself a leader under construction. Always learning. Always adapting. The vignette by the authors that describes that "not all individuals come to the table with the same amount of food on their plate" is a powerful representation of the ongoing learning we all need to embrace and which should be fueled by an endless curiosity and a desire to improve our individual knowledge of what works and what doesn't when we serve as leaders. My greatest leadership teachers have been sourced from unlikely places and include less than enlightened managers, failed projects, and my own missteps as I learned through experiences too numerous to mention. Over the years, books that integrated key theories and approaches to developing my own leadership style were few and far between and often yielded little benefit to my individual development. Rather than a new leader having to retrace my path, *There Is No Box* can be an important foundation to building a leader's approach to relatable leadership and establishing themselves as an influencer.

There Is No Box not only resets the approach to leadership but redefines the key characteristics that all leaders need to embrace as they navigate a post pandemic world. Characteristics that Simon and Marisa outline such as the ability to mentor, being collaborative, and authenticity are vital dimensions that we all need to incorporate into our approach supporting our teams while navigating an ever-complex geopolitical environment that seemingly shifts by the day. Being a relatable leader, which is core to the authors' methodology to establishing your leadership style, takes situational leadership theory to a new level not previously seen in recent literature. A relatable leader is one who aligns their value system—their why— and shows up every day for their team knowing they won't have all the answers. Instead, the leader realizes the act of being present and authentic is the first step in creating a circle where all are invited to share their concerns, their fears, and their challenges. Yes please! It is also important to note that Simon and Marisa are not suggesting that being a relatable leader means that you will be liked by all. In fact, hard decisions will still need to be made by leaders; however, the brilliant linkages in this book between project management, communication, and compassionate approaches model how you can intersect with your team while allowing those difficult decisions to be understood and respected.

There Is No Box shows us all the ways to step outside of our comfort zone, embrace ambiguity, and leverage our experiences of immovable boundaries and rigid playbooks to create a new paradigm between a leader and those they influence. Make no mistake: Once you are outside of the box, you will periodically turn back and reflect upon your time in the box, but Marisa and Simon gently turn our sight towards the limitless possibilities that exist on the horizon. That horizon of possibility not only challenges each of us to be at our best as we encounter new unknowns, but more importantly, those infinite opportunities will be instrumental in our creation of our next generation of leaders. Our future leaders will author their own definition of what it means to be outside of the box. In fact, our future leaders, by leveraging this book, will redefine for all of us what leadership outside of the box truly means in the decades to come.

—Mary Ludden, MBA, PhD
Senior Vice Chancellor and Senior Vice Provost
Northeastern University

PREFACE

You have exactly one life in which to do
everything you'll ever do. Act accordingly.

Colin Wright
Author, *Act Accordingly*

Simon and I have dedicated our almost three decades together to living a life guided by curiosity. Many years ago we reached the point when our opinions and our pictures of happiness aligned, illuminating for us how it was that we wanted to live our lives. This realization came at a low point in my day when he said to me, "Life isn't something you have to do. Life is something you get to do." From that moment, I realized that I didn't have to stay in a job that didn't add value to my day. But what else did I want to do in this one short and unpredictable existence on Earth?

In my opinion, Simon's outlook on life makes him one of the greatest philosophers of our time. He's right. Life is something we get to do, and there's so much we *could* do. I left the office and entered the classroom, where I taught high school students language arts and coached the cheerleading and dance teams. Simon became a project manager for some global corporations and then for a local government. We'd both enjoyed our time in graduate school, and he wanted to return for his PhD, which eventually led him to higher education administration. After about a decade, I left the classroom, earned my EdD, and pursued my dream of working in the publishing industry.

But we still ask ourselves what else we want to do. Combining that inquiry with our insatiable curiosity, we had the perfect recipe for research. Over the years, we've merged our interests and researched different topics. One concept kept resurfacing—the idea that there is no box. But what does that even mean?

To us, it means not settling for what others have chosen as the default standard. It means that instead of doubting yourself when you wonder if you could do something that might seem out of reach, you think *why not?*

Any of us who have had jobs have had bosses. People with titles like supervisor, manager, or director. But have you had the opportunity to work with a leader? Bosses are not always leaders, and vice versa. Simon and I have studied leadership since our twenties, and it really bothered us that we couldn't name more than a handful of good leaders between the two of us. Why hadn't we had the opportunity to work with more effective leaders during our careers?

Fortunately, we have worked with some bosses who were also fantastic leaders. As we engaged more with other leaders in different industries, our beliefs were challenged and we grew in ways we never imagined. Most notably, we witnessed the power of a certain type of leader—the relatable leader.

Relatable leaders are essential because they understand that there is no box. They understand everyone has their own journey to get to where they want to be, and they don't expect everyone to follow the same path. And once we understood that concept, we found our *why not.*

A while ago I tweeted, "When you reach the point in your life where you're living your dream, I hope you remember to appreciate the path you traveled to get there. Then, if you're able, help someone else on their path." Our ambition in life is to help others find and travel their paths.

There is no one way to make it, whatever *make it* even means. It's all relative because success looks different for everyone. You're never too late or too old to achieve your goals, and your goals can change over time. You're not stuck on one track. There is not just one path to get to where you want to be. And this is a stunningly spectacular fact.

INTRODUCTION

> If they don't give you a seat at the
> table, bring in a folding chair.
> **Shirley Chisholm**
> **First African American woman in Congress**

There are so many great leadership books out there that describe strategies for enhancing leadership styles. Those books have led us to where we are right now—with a firm belief in the value of sharing what we've learned. We could've said the world doesn't need another leadership book. But we believe the world needs *this* leadership book. Why? This book will show you how to become a relatable leader, and relatable leaders can change the world. We believe leaders are capable of improving the human condition. Great leaders are capable of generating a joy and love for life among those who get to work with them. Their feelings radiate into other aspects of their lives and influences the lives of those around them.

We believe leadership skills can be taught; you can learn how to be an effective leader who has an impact on those around you. My career is firmly grounded in project management, and I find referencing project management concepts to be useful in my everyday life. So you'll see me reference them as we move through this book.

Since we believe education and books change lives and that knowledge is the greatest equalizer, we're merging leadership theories with leadership practices in this book to help you become an enhanced version of yourself and actively participate in ongoing leadership development.

One common theme we noticed during our research of leaders—and in our own experiences with leading—is how relatability broadens the range of influence. Our purpose is to help you focus on the benefits of being relatable and, by becoming a relatable leader, generate more joy and love for life—not just your professional life but your life as a whole. If everything really does start at the top, then leaders shape the mood and tone every day. A relatable leader's influence reaches beyond the workplace.

Leadership isn't a trait. Leadership is a lifestyle and should be ingrained in our core. The way we lead shouldn't be a competency that we pull out when we're in front of our teams or our stakeholders. The way we lead should come from inside ourselves and be a part of every moment.

Since we believe that leadership and influence are related, all leadership starts with self-influence. This means more than just how you view yourself, but also how that view of yourself correlates with your thoughts and actions. In what ways can you influence yourself to become an effective leader? To that end, as you enter *There Is No Box*, you'll see a mixture of anecdotes, interviews, and examples broken into three parts all revolving around one focus: you.

This book is based on the idea that you are the CEO of your life. This concept is something that will be repeated throughout the book, so take a moment and promote yourself to CEO of your life right now. You are not a bystander in your life. You are in charge. You have the final say in every decision you make. When you take responsibility as the CEO of your life, you are acknowledging that you are the leader of your life, and, therefore, it is your actions that will determine what type of life you will lead. As the CEO of your life, just like professional CEOs, you have a team of people around you, and the ways in which you relate to those people impact your life and theirs.

Since this is a practical guide for the relatable leader, we're hoping that means you intend to cultivate your relatability by examining where you start, how you're influenced, and ways to break down those boundaries—self-imposed or otherwise—to becoming a meaningful leader in your own life and in the lives of those influenced by you.

Relatable leaders cultivate their relatability in five ways:

1. They know their starting lines.
2. They increase their cultural agility.
3. They practice compassionate communication.
4. They embrace the leadership lifestyle.
5. They view leadership as nonhierarchical.

As you move through the book, you'll find three parts focusing on these five strategies to becoming a relatable leader.

Part one focuses on what Marisa and I have learned as we've studied leadership and taken on leadership roles. We're told to color inside the lines, and those lines include preset definitions. This is where we'll examine commonly taught definitions of leadership and leadership theories, allowing you to reflect on your own leadership examples. We'll also explore the complexity of becoming a relatable leader and our interconnectedness with other people within our personal and professional lives.

Part two explores the five ways relatable leaders cultivate their relatability, and we'll break these down into strategies for cultivating your own relatability. We're going to look at what you already know, such as who you are and where you come from. From birth, we're exposed to experiences that make up who we are. We learn the rules that define how we interact with the world around us and where we fit into our different groups: family, friends, classmates, colleagues, and acquaintances.

When we enter the workforce, we may find our bosses asking us to think outside the box. This is the time when we expand what we know. We use the new influences around us to create new ideas and broaden our understanding of what it means to be a leader. When you think outside the box, you find new ways to examine your life and your leadership development by exploring some new concepts such as cultural agility, compassionate communication, and nonhierarchical leadership. We'll also dive into how relatable leaders engage in their communities through community leadership.

In part three, we'll address the concept that there is no box—that there is not just one path for getting where you want to go. Everyone's journey to becoming an effective leader is different because everyone starts with different advantages and obstacles. You should have a plan to help you discover ways to increase your influence by cultivating your relatability. With examples and exercises on how to create your unique leadership development plan, you'll be able to create a path to becoming a relatable leader.

We have seen amazing results from relatable leaders, and this book is for leaders who want an honest glimpse into how to enhance their worldview and broaden their range of influence.

We're excited to be a part of your leadership development. And we hope this book helps you become an effective and relatable leader.

PART ONE
Color Inside the Lines

During childhood, we're taught to color inside the lines. Eat your vegetables. Drink eight glasses of water a day. Sit up straight. Learn the rules. Follow the leader. Know your place. These aren't bad rules. After all, they establish what is considered acceptable behavior for existing in society. There's a purpose for learning how to color inside the lines. By giving children crayons or markers and asking them to color inside a given shape, children are not only improving their fine motor skills, but they are also learning about boundaries. Pablo Picasso said, "Learn the rules like a pro. Break them like an artist."

Once you know the rules, you can use them as a framework for forming new rules. Once you as a leader know the established leadership styles and theories, you can use them to your advantage as you become your best leader self. In part one we look at what is relatable leadership, level the playing field by providing an overview of leadership styles and theories, and explore the complexity of relatability and leadership.

1 What Is Relatable Leadership?

Many leaders aren't born with a natural ability to lead. They don't all possess the traits and competencies great leadership books tell us are needed to be an effective leader. These books tend to break leadership skills into three categories: administrative, interpersonal, and conceptual. We're not discounting that. Not at all. In fact, our shelves are filled with informative and motivational books that helped us form our definition and opinion of leaders and leadership. But leadership isn't always a one-size-fits-all scenario.

We studied, practiced, and used quantitative, qualitative, and action research to further our own understanding of leadership and figure out our leadership styles. In doing so, we put a name to the concept of when leaders combine the best elite methodologies to create the best and most applicable outcome. We've combined all those words that make an effective leader into one descriptor: relatable. What is relatable leadership? In this chapter we're going to look at how leadership and relatability align by providing

* a definition of relatable leadership,
* a list of traits of relatable leaders,

* prerequisites for becoming a leader, and
* a reflection upon why you want to be a leader.

Relatability works in two ways for effective leaders: relating to others and relating to circumstances. When you can relate to others, you adjust your communication style so they can relate to you. If people can't understand you—or relate to you—then your message won't matter. Relatable leaders focus on getting their message to those who need it, and they understand that it's up to them to make sure their message is received. Relatable leaders focus more on how they can be beneficial to others rather than wonder how others can benefit them. In other words, relatable leaders bring value to the lives of others. When you can relate to circumstances, you adjust your demeanor to fit the situation. Relatable leaders match their approach to fit the scenario. For example, they understand how their attitude during a recession would need to be different from their style in a time of organizational growth. Relatable leaders have gained a variety of different experiences and can apply the lessons learned from those experiences to relate to new circumstances. In other words, relatable leaders know how to read the room.

Relatable leadership entails understanding different leadership styles and being able to move fluidly within the style that's appropriate for the situation. It's being able to adjust seamlessly to the person you're dealing with or the situation you're leading.

TRAITS OF RELATABLE LEADERS

* Authentic
* Compassionate
* Collaborative

* Communicative
* Culturally agile
* Mentoring
* Optimistic
* Persistent
* Resilient
* Self-aware
* Self-accepting
* Service-oriented
* Sustainability-focused

Oprah Winfrey is quoted as saying, "I wanted to be a teacher. And to be known for inspiring my students to be more than they thought they could be." Would it interest you to know that relatable leadership can be taught? Being able to read the situation and act accordingly for the best interest of your team can be taught, and this means that anyone who wants to be a relatable leader can be.

John Meyer, president of Hodges University, taught leadership courses, which were obligatory in all management curricula, for twelve years. We reached out to him to get his perspective on leadership, on our idea that leadership can be taught and learned, and on the value of relatable leadership. He reinforced our belief that leadership is a relationship built on influence. Further, he noted that teaching leadership theory and having students take notes, spit back theories verbatim, and select a theory that they most identify with is different from teaching someone how to be a leader. Ultimately, he agreed that leadership can be taught—"with stipulations." Even if an effective leader and teacher teaches someone the leadership styles and theories and shows them case studies of how best to behave in certain situations, those leadership actions will only be learned under certain conditions. You can learn all about leadership, but that doesn't make you a leader.

How does one learn to lead?

THREE PREREQUISITES FOR BECOMING A LEADER

If you're interested in learning how to become a leader, there are three prerequisites that you should have before embarking on this journey. We've adapted them from the stipulations Meyer suggested:

1. **You should want to influence people.** All leadership starts with self-leadership, so the first person you should want to influence is yourself. But beyond you, one prerequisite for learning how to be a leader is your own willingness to influence others. Sometimes people get pushed into leadership roles, but without the willingness and desire to influence others, their effectiveness as a leader will be lacking. How much enthusiasm do we really put into something we don't want to do?

2. **You should believe that you have the ability to influence people.** If you don't believe you can influence others, how can you expect them to be influenced by you?

3. **You should care.** This is perhaps the most important prerequisite to learning how to lead. When we care about something, our passion radiates from our core. This passion sparks excitement, and others will want to be part of whatever it is that you care about. You should also care about people. Leaders need to care about those around them.

Once you have these three prerequisites, you can begin your journey to learning how to become a relatable leader.

BECOMING A RELATABLE LEADER

Relatable leaders cultivate their relatability in five ways:

1. They know their starting lines.
2. They increase their cultural agility.
3. They practice compassionate communication.
4. They embrace the leadership lifestyle.
5. They view leadership as nonhierarchical.

We'll address these five strategies, which you can use to cultivate your own relatability on the following two premises:

1. **Relatability broadens your range of influence.** As you begin your leadership journey, you will have the opportunity to influence others, hopefully in meaningful and value-added ways. Through cultivating your own relatability, you will be able to build better relationships with a wider range of people than those in your immediate circle. Learning how to become a relatable leader depends on your willingness to cultivate your own relatability through the five ways we'll explore in part two.

2. **You are the CEO of your life.** Once you accept that you are the final decision maker for every aspect of your life, and you understand the responsibility that encompasses that acceptance, you will view all your actions and decisions through the lens of being a leader with the ability to influence others. As a CEO, your actions affect more than just yourself, and fully comprehending the ways in which you can improve the lives of others is a powerful realization.

CHAPTER ONE REFLECTION

This book is written for those who want an honest glimpse into how to enhance their perspective of their lives and how their personal and professional lives are interconnected. The very title, *There Is No Box,* suggests that there is no one way to do something. The boundaries we've placed on ourselves are just that—ideas we've accepted as an ordinary part of life. But in this book you'll be asked to reframe how you consider an issue or think about a certain topic.

For example, a manager once told me to separate my personal feelings from my professional opinion on a business decision. The truth is I knew what he was asking, but I couldn't do it. In that situation, what was considered a professionally responsible business choice went against my personal feelings that the decision was just wrong. My personal feelings influenced my professional opinion because as I developed my own leadership style, I realized that even in business, even with bottom lines, we're interacting with humans.

The point of many leadership books is to provide a framework to become a better, more effective leader, and that means change. Hopefully, you will feel yourself changing as you read through these chapters and become more aware of who you are. And as you change, you will see how you can become a change agent who can influence others in positive ways.

In this chapter's reflection, we'd like you to take a moment to consider the three prerequisites for becoming a leader and focus on the third: you should care. Think about what you care about. It could be a concept or an issue. It could be your family, your career, the growth and success of your organization, your students if you're a teacher, the environment, pet adoption, and so on. It can be anything you want it to be. Now complete this phrase out loud or in the silence of your mind, and write it down:

I want to be a leader because I care about . . .

2 Leveling the Playing Field

Every journey to somewhere starts somewhere. The first time I lectured for Georgetown University's McDonough School of Business's MBA students, I realized the significance of an uneven playing field. The course was on troubled projects, but more than that, it was a course on preparing the students to be better leaders for when they joined and helmed a leadership team. The course did more than show them ways in which they would work better in teams and how to communicate with shareholders about correcting a troubled project. It showed them how leadership is not a competency; leadership is a lifestyle.

I entered the lecture hall with one frame of mind but exited with a much deeper understanding of privilege. I'd mistakenly categorized all those MBA students as privileged—starting the course on the same page. After all, they'd read the course description. They'd registered for the class on troubled projects. They must know what a project is, what project managers do, and the importance of leadership on a project team, right?

Not so much.

Some did. For others, this was the first time they were introduced to project management. They stopped by my desk after class to seek clarification, and I took their questions to heart and learned from my assumptions. Not everyone comes to the table with the same amount of food on their plate. Not everyone enters a classroom with the same amount of knowledge. It was up to me to create the starting line for the class. Since it was an elective graduate course, I had to find a way to level the playing field so those without any experience in project management and those who had been out of a classroom setting for up to a decade could make sense of the case studies and examples that others with experience in project management already understood.

After almost a decade of teaching undergraduate and graduate students, I'm convinced of two facts: education can level any playing field, and when you take charge of your own development as the CEO of your life, you actively seek knowledge to help you level any playing field. Those students took the initiative to further their understanding by engaging with me after class. If they hadn't, I wouldn't have expanded my worldview either. As a teacher I've learned that I can learn from students in unexpected ways. Because of this, I believe in education for all, but not the same education for everyone. Not everyone may have the time or money to earn a graduate degree in leadership or an MBA, but everyone who wants to learn more about leadership and leadership development could have access to books.

In this chapter, we're not going to assume anything. We're going to level the playing field by providing

* an overview of leadership,
* a table of leadership styles,
* a discussion about relatable leadership,
* the benefits of being relatable, and
* a reflection on relatable leadership.

UNDERSTANDING LEADERSHIP

Many people agree or at least see the relationship leadership has with influence. The ways in which a leader can influence others determines how successful the leader will be at achieving their goals. Effective leaders use strategies to influence and gain support from others. This being the case, a leader's ability to influence is essential for success—personal and professional. Without leadership, without someone making decisions, there would be no forward momentum. Even families and friend groups need someone to take charge. Without leadership, companies would not meet their objectives to deliver products and services to their customers. The world needs leaders who are willing to use their ability to influence others to improve the world. But there are many kinds of leaders.

As we mentioned in the introduction, any of us who have had jobs have had bosses, people with such titles as supervisor, manager, or director. But we haven't all had the opportunity to work with a leader. Bosses are not always leaders, and vice versa. As with managerial styles, literature identifies a myriad of leadership styles. Over the years, you might have read or heard about numerous concepts related to leadership, its meaning, and its approach. Rather than rehash these lessons, I want to focus on several interesting leadership theories that helped me discover there is no one best way to lead. In fact, the leaders I've learned the most from have been those who have combined different leadership styles depending on whether their organizations were in growth mode or undergoing downsizing. Ultimately, these theories broadened my understanding of the skills and qualities of effective leaders, but the variations among the different styles and seeing them in action solidified what it takes to be an effective leader.

Many years ago, I worked for someone who could only be described as a laissez-faire leader. These leaders do not try to enforce control over their employees. This particular style rarely has any positive effect on employee development, often leading to unmotivated employees. This individual I worked for couldn't care less about how we ran our department or whether any changes that we introduced had a high impact on our software systems. These types of leaders display a lack of presence with their employees and avoid rewarding their subordinates. This often leads to the development of role ambiguity for the employee since the expectations of their supervisor is not clearly defined. Furthermore, laissez-faire leaders delay action, in most circumstances avoiding doing anything, and are known as nonleaders.

In contrast, my boss's boss was strictly authoritarian. This boss was someone who constantly needed to exert his influence and control over the most minute tasks, but he rarely participated in group discussions or addressed group questions. His micromanagement style prevented any meaningful participation. (I have, however, been in situations where the authoritarian leadership style worked well, such as when initially facing a crisis management scenario.) Neither leader was aware of the types of changes my group was responsible for, which was a blessing as well as a curse.

Reflecting on these previous leaders helped me develop my own leadership style. At first I characterized my leadership preference as democratic. Why? Because of how I approached change with my team. I focused on one concept and thought it could define my leadership style. While it is not easy to make most changes within an organization, democratic leaders can build collaboration and foster support among employees through intrinsic motivation, and this was what I hoped to accomplish with my team.

Regardless of styles, I learned as a leader that many factors prevent change from occurring. For example, a lack of employee engagement and effective communication at one point hindered my efforts to institute change. As a democratic leader, I understood that my employees resisted big changes because they preferred their routines and often knew what to expect. Some of the unexpected changes that occurred in my environment created a sense of uneasiness and discomfort among my employees. As a result, effective communication is one of the factors I continue building on when making any change. I learned that my team appreciated being told not only what was changing, but also why it was changing. Leaders should not expect employees to hear about a major change and immediately adjust to the new circumstances.

Effective leaders practice good communication, especially when it comes to why rules and policies are changing, how the new ones will be better, and if there are consequences for failing to adapt to the change. This communication, as I've come to learn, shows the team that the leader cares about them and how they perceive the changes.

It's essential for everyone on the team to have a stake in the changes that affect them. As a leader, I had to learn how frequently to follow up with each of my team members, especially during times of change. It was important to me that everyone's voice and opinion were heard. Even if a member had nothing to share, I encouraged them to reflect on what others had shared. I found that this simple approach fostered collaboration over the long run, as team members understood that I cared about their opinions.

This example shows why I first classified my leadership style as democratic. Back then I led with the belief that the first step to building trust was through open communication. Now I can safely deduct that leadership qualities adapt to the demands of the external environment. I've come to understand that certain theories do not transcend all scenarios. The bottom line is leaders must find a middle ground where their subordinates are not micromanaged but are consulted through rich communication and collaboration.

Just as my previous bosses' leadership styles showed me how I did and didn't want to lead, the following leadership styles will act as a foundation upon which you can form your own comparisons about the leaders you've worked with or read about, as well as generate opinions for which type of leader you think you might have been or you want to be in any given situation. Maybe you've read articles about each style or maybe these are theories you haven't heard of before. Either way, we want to set the foundation for you to have a working knowledge of the leadership theories and styles that we've encountered in our graduate courses, in popular thought-leader magazines, and in the real world.

These leadership styles are not mutually exclusive. Becoming a relatable leader entails knowing how to take advantage of all these competencies and applying them to the situation at hand in order to enable a positive outcome. Different leadership styles provide more effective results in certain conditions and circumstances. Table 1 provides an overview of some of the more established leadership styles.

As you read through the table, we'd like you to consider the following questions in relation to your personality, the types of organizations you've been a part of, and your specific industry:

* Have you had any bosses who have used this style?
* How did you like working with someone who used this style?
* Do you think you use this style of leadership?
* In what situations would this style of leadership work well?

After you've read through the table, we'll address how four of these styles apply to being a relatable leader.

TABLE 1 Leadership Styles

Leadership Theory/Style	Summation
Adaptive Leadership	The adaptive leadership theory explains that authentic leaders are persistent, methodical, and able to accept disequilibrium and discomfort.[1] Adaptive leaders are • most adept at resolving conflict, • specific about their expectations, • respectful and understanding when they need to explain to their employees that their behaviors are disruptive and need to change, • clear and consistent with their feedback and explain the consequences when an unacceptable behavior doesn't change, • willing to provide second chances for their employees through job rotation, job enlargement, or job enrichment, and • courageous and confront people in a fair-minded way.
Authentic Leadership	Researchers suggest that authentic leaders are self-aware, mission driven, and focused on long-term results.[2] Authentic leaders are • committed to bettering themselves, • self-aware, • disciplined, • mission driven, and • inspirers of faith.[3]
Charismatic Leadership	Researchers found that charismatic leadership involves charm and the personality of the leader. Charismatic leaders are • able to inspire others, • committed to their vision, • sensitive to those around them, and • willing to take risks.

Leadership Theory/Style	Summation
Coaching Leadership	The coaching leadership style relies on a collaborative effort between the leader and their team, giving the team a more empowered role in the relationship. Coaching leaders are • collaborative, • empathetic, • encouraging, • motivating, and • supportive.
Democratic Leadership	Democratic leadership is best used with experienced teams who have the knowledge and motivation to contribute when in a team environment. Democratic leaders are • focused on collaboration, • more concerned with building a consensus, and • looking for the team's input.
Inspiring Leadership	Inspiring leadership focuses on building others up and encouraging them to reach their full potential. Inspiring leaders are • committed to values, • encourage personal development, • inclusive, • inspiring, and • relationship builders.
Servant Leadership	Servant leadership stems from a leader's willingness to serve at the individual, team, organizational, and community levels. Servant leaders are • caring, • empathetic, • humble, and • unselfish.

Leadership Theory/Style	Summation
Situational Leadership	The situational leadership theory states that no one leadership style fits all, and different leadership styles are needed depending on the situation. Situational leaders are • adaptive, • flexible, • observant, and • responsive.
Strategic Leadership	Strategic leadership focuses on finding ways an organization can improve and convincing others to change. Strategic leaders are • change oriented, • delegators, • future focused, • open-minded, and • problem solvers.
Transformational Leadership	Transformational leaders focus on personal and professional growth for themselves and those around them. Transformational leaders are • change agents, • encouraging, • engaging, • inspiring, • motivating, and • supportive.

BEING RELATABLE: AUTHENTIC, INSPIRING, SERVANT, AND TRANSFORMATIONAL LEADERSHIP

The romance of leadership theory, which describes the tendency to see leadership as the determining factor of an organization's success, provides an explanation for our need to label individuals responsible for actions, decisions, and outcomes. However, leadership and the way leadership has been defined and viewed is shifting. This is a result of the global economy, social media, and industry progress, and leadership competencies bridge the theories as we redefine and solidify leadership as both a noun and an adjective. Table 1 focuses on the positive connotations of those leadership styles. The four styles that apply to the ways relatable leaders cultivate their relatability are authentic leadership, inspiring leadership, servant leadership, and transformational leadership.

In one of my previous organizations, I often witnessed situations where leaders demonstrated a lack of humility, respect, and partnership with their team members. Each of these three factors distinguish the artificial leader from authentic leaders.

Authentic leadership theory is focused on the leaders who are driven by the mission and final outcomes of that mission while exhibiting self-awareness. This self-awareness correlates with how well relatable leaders know their starting lines. They know where they come from and how they are positioned among those around them. In fact, authentic leaders have achieved authenticity through self-awareness, self-acceptance, and authentic actions and relationships. Such leaders seek to strengthen their relationships with employees by focusing on transparency, trust, guidance toward worthy objectives, and follower development.

The inspiring leader is perceived by others to be someone who has knowledge and sensitivity to the problems that need to be addressed.

An inspiring leader is not someone who micromanages and forces others to follow, but is the one who guides.[4] One of the most distinct qualities of inspiring leaders is their passion to help others. In addition to having this passion, inspiring leaders are also competent leaders. Competence is a kind of thirst for knowledge and self-improvement that demonstrates skills needed to overcome challenges. Finally, a key quality for inspiring leaders is mentorship. This quality instills in a leader the necessary drive to guide, mentor, and provide feedback to others to help them see their actions from another perspective. Furthermore, this quality helps leaders build trust with their employees through feedback and guidance. Inspiring leaders understand the importance of encouraging personal development and building relationships with others.

A desire to help others is also associated with servant leadership. Servant leaders take the development of their employees as essential, so they engage in support and guidance while fostering the development of a trusting and genuine community. This community focuses on open dialogue and listening to their team to discover their needs first. Servant leaders practice compassionate communication, which puts the followers' needs first and creates a culture of altruism; the focus is on others rather than on personal ideas and desires. This in turn reduces the conflict among team members. Servant leaders focus on the investment in the betterment of their teams by adopting the values of inspiration, equality, community incorporation, and guidance.

Servant leadership is guiding and supporting, understanding, being genuine, developing relationships, and building a community.[5] By investing in employees, servant leaders encourage and support their employees to focus on their successes instead of the leader's success. Servant leadership focuses on team-building models. Servant leaders are effective in helping their employees adapt to change by learning how the employees process things. Then together, they can work on ways to integrate better within the organization.

Transformational leaders focus on transforming their teams and on tasks that help them understand what motivates and influences employees. As agents of change, transformational leaders help employees understand strategy and how to assess value over numbers. Just as relatable leaders view leadership as nonhierarchical, transformational leaders seek leadership from everyone on their team. By encouraging everyone on their team to transform into the best version of themselves, each person, including the leader, learns, grows, and experiences new opportunities.

THE BENEFITS OF BEING RELATABLE

We often form our opinions based on whether we want to be more or less like a particular something. For example, you see a Maserati speeding down the highway and think, *slow down* or *I wish I was in a Maserati speeding down the highway.* You see your boss do something ridiculous and might think, *when I'm a boss, I'm going to be able to do that ridiculous thing, too* or *when I'm a boss, I won't act that way.* Similarly, you will instinctively lean toward one leadership methodology.

Learning when and in what ways to incorporate other leadership approaches will allow you to tap into the relatable leadership approach in ways other leaders might not be able to. Since leadership has a relationship with influence, the more people you can relate to and who can relate to you, the more likely you'll be able to communicate your message and influence them.

There are pros and cons to all leadership styles, depending on the situation. As I've mentioned, I started my career aspiring to live by the democratic leadership style. Earlier in her teaching career, my wife wanted to be an inspiring leader, whereas some people classify her as a servant leader. But as any personality type indicator test shows, we are not 100 percent any one thing. We are a mosaic of all the little experiences we've had in our lives, which is why it is critical for us to understand our positionality—the perspective from which we understand the world. It gives us a starting point for understanding why we think the way we do and why we are where we are in our life right now. Every decision, interpretation, and reaction we make is from our own point of view, and no one else has the exact same perspective as you.

It's never too late to become the type of leader you want to be. Choosing to be a relatable leader has more benefits than a bulleted list can convey. Still, for those who like lists, here is a limited list of the key benefits of becoming a relatable leader:

* Broadens your range of influence
* Helps you focus on understanding your journey and how it fits within the journey of those around you
* Helps you develop lasting relationships through connections with others and by building trust among diverse groups
* Helps you understand the importance of giving to those around you, within your organizations, and communities in solution-driven ways
* Helps you engage in positive change to set the atmosphere for purposeful and fulfilled living
* Helps you become an enhanced version of yourself
* Gives you the tools to help someone else become an enhanced version of themselves
* Helps you explore your leadership style through actively participating in an ongoing leadership development process

On a micro level, relatability holds you accountable for your actions and how those actions are perceived by those around you. As you become more relatable, you learn to check yourself by asking, and answering, why you are doing something and for what reasons.

These little self-checks help you develop your sense of place among everyone else in your life such as your family, your friends, and those within your organization, community, and other groups.

On the macro level, relatability improves your sense of common ground with others. It makes it easier for others to get along with you and follow your lead.

The greatest benefit of being relatable is the ease in which you function within the world.

CHAPTER TWO REFLECTION

Just like learning to color inside the lines, these first chapters set the foundation for your leadership development. Before we move into the complexity of being a leader, we'd like you to reflect on the milestones you've already achieved.

In this chapter's reflection, we'd like you to take a moment to consider your accomplishments. Remind yourself that whether big or small, memorable or seemingly insignificant, you've already achieved so much even though it might feel as if you missed the mark, even though it might feel as if there isn't hope for a different outcome. You're here, reading and learning and growing. You're here with us at the end of this chapter, and that means you're ready for the next steps on your leadership development journey. But before you move on, we'd like you to take the time to marvel at your accomplishments.

Now complete this phrase out loud or in the silence of your mind, and write it down:

I'm glad to have accomplished . . .

3 The Complexity of Relatability

Relatable leadership draws upon a holistic view of the individual and has a sharp focus on choosing the appropriate methodology to gain the most successful results within particular situations. A relatable leader is a person everyone feels they know, can relate to, and trust in most situations. Becoming that person is complex.

Beyond leaders being able to relate to others, leaders need to be able to shift into different modes so others can better relate to them. Becoming a relatable leader is a complex process. When I first started on my leadership journey, I felt as if I were being pulled in too many directions to know if I was on the right track. But as I gained more experience and saw how everything is interconnected, becoming relatable became less complex.

In this chapter, we're going to explore how to make sense of the complexity of relatability by providing

* an overview of systems and complexity,
* an exploration of the ways organizations benefit from relatable leaders,

* an explanation for how human behavior plays a role in complexity,
* a discussion on the importance of stakeholders,
* strategies for handling the complexity of leadership, and
* a reflection upon your effect on your many systems.

Complexity theory recognizes that there is specific but shared order and behavior among systems. This theory attempts to explain such behaviors since the usual rules of nature are not sufficient to do so. Moreover, the theory rationalizes how separate elements of a system interact with one another to impact the system.

To understand the concept of systems, we need answers to a few questions: What laws does the system obey? What are its substances? What external entities may interact with it?

One example is a human being. You are made up of organs, which are separate systems that work independently as well as with the larger system of your whole body. As a person, you are part of a family, which is also a system because each person in the family acts independently and is also interrelated with other members of the family. You are part of an organization as well. When you're with your family, you act within the definition of your label: son, brother, father, daughter, sister, or mother. The same is true at work, where your job title helps define your role within your team or department and within the organization.

Why is understanding leadership through this systems lens important? Because relatable leaders understand their leadership is not singular to them. Their actions are observed by others, and what they do has the potential to affect others in ways they may never see. They are able to seamlessly shift among interconnected systems.

COMPLEX FORCES

When leaders understand how they're operating within a complex system, they're better able to devise approaches to lead effectively. This understanding gives their actions greater meaning because they focus on how their behavior can influence the lives of those around them. As a relatable leader, you position yourself within the hierarchy of systems with the realization that your behaviors and decisions affect all the systems of which you are a part, including

* you,
* your family,
* your colleagues within a team or department,
* your colleagues within the entire organization,
* any teams, groups, or club members,
* your neighbors, and
* your community.

Why is this important for our leadership discussion? Organizations are complex adaptive systems. Therefore, they are constantly changing. Effective leaders promote internal dynamics that allow for adapting to unknown futures, such as encouraging fluidity and fostering collaboration and communication. Relatable leaders shift gears during change and view long-term planning and development as a spontaneous, self-organizing process that leads to new opportunities. In Project Management Institute's *Pulse of the Profession In-Depth Report: Navigating Complexity*, over half of the surveyed CEOs reported doubt that their organizations are prepared to manage the complexity in their organizations, while four out of five CEOs foresaw increases of the current level of complexity in their organizations during the next five years.[1]

Leadership requires the provision of active executive sponsorship and commitment. It also involves empowering others within the organization with the support to facilitate successful delivery of results. Leadership also involves awareness of any early warning signs of problems and the enactment of action plans to address potential dangers.

Every action taken should contribute to the betterment of the entire system. Collaboration among all the systems enhances the health of the entire system. By understanding all the complex forces influencing a system, relatable leaders move within all their systems with a fluidity that keeps all the systems moving forward. Without that conscious realization, any one of the many complex systems in proximity to the leader could lose their momentum.

ORGANIZATIONAL COMPLEXITY

Even when relatable leaders understand how they fit within multiple complex systems, they will experience other systems of varying degrees of complexity. After all, we interact with people almost everywhere, and those people interact with different people and within different systems. One space that occupies a majority of our time is the workplace.

Organizational structures often influence the success of the organization. If you're an entrepreneur, the way you structure your organization is something to consider from the start. Some of the most common organizational structures are functional, divisional, and line. There are more organizational structures, but these three provide a nice overview for showing how the structure can influence how a leader can best lead.

Within a functional organizational structure, the departments are divided by work type such as finance, marketing, and production. Leaders within a functional organization should consider how to strengthen bonds and increase the flow of communication among the departments, especially since each department may be dependent on another department to complete their work. For example, if someone in the marketing department is dependent on someone in the finance department to approve a work order, then the finance department may delay the approval, thereby delaying the marketing person's ability to complete their job successfully.

The divisional organization has divisions that operate in silos, where each division has its own finance, marketing, and production teams. This type of an organization promotes a team culture, where each team has its own resources and is not dependent on other divisions to complete its work. But divisional organization can also breed unhealthy competition among the divisions if those division leaders are not led by someone who wants the best overall success for the organization.

In a line organization, the hierarchy is linear from top to bottom and is characterized by the vertical relationship and simple boss-to-subordinate structure. This allows for a clear definition of who is responsible for what and to whom a person directly reports. The military is an example of a line organization.

As we've mentioned before, we don't believe there is one leadership style to fit all the infinite circumstances that leaders may face. Relatable leaders who know what type of organization they are leading can better understand how to bring their leadership team together and focus on ways to spotlight the strengths and minimize the weaknesses within that type of organization. Execution of programs and projects designed to move an organization forward can be hindered by a lack of flexibility from leaders who don't understand that the organizational structure is another component of the complexity of leading. As you gain a greater understanding of the role of a relatable leader, you'll see how being part of a complex system requires leaders to be flexible.

HUMAN BEHAVIOR AND COMPLEXITY

Human behavior plays a significant role in complexity and how a leader deals with others within complex systems. The main source of complexity arises from the effect of both individual and group behaviors within a system.

As a younger project manager forming my first team, I made the mistake of hiring for skills instead of personality, and I ended up managing personalities instead of the project. As I developed a sense of what kind of leader I wanted to be, I formed the opinion that it's better to hire for personality. I can teach the skills to the person with the right attitude. This is also why I love higher education. At the graduate level, I'm afforded the opportunity to work with adults who come into the master's program with the mindset that they want to learn, and they want to earn a graduate degree in the process. They already have the right attitude, so I can guide them through learning new competencies.

Still, even when someone has the right attitude, leaders need to be aware of the conditions that lead to complexity among humans. These conditions can be present within personal and professional interactions, and the place where you might observe them with the most frequency is within an organization and within a team. When leaders keep these potential conditions in mind, they will be ready to mitigate any issues that occur because of the complexity among humans. The conditions that lead to complexity are

* unrealistic expectations,
* lack of clarity regarding the goals, decision-making processes, and outcomes among key stakeholders, and
* hidden agendas among key decision makers.

Unrealistic expectations develop when there's mismanagement of what is expected. Whether they're in our personal or professional lives, these unrealistic expectations occur because of miscommunication. Leaders can't immediately tell what their team might be expecting during specific interactions, but relatable leaders prepare their team to manage expectations from the start.

When key stakeholders lack clarity about the goals, decision-making processes, and outcomes, members of the team may make their own assumptions about what to do and how to do it. Relatable leaders proactively address ambiguous direction at the beginning of any interaction with their team.

Hidden agendas among key decision makers can occur when they have opposing motivations for supporting or opposing something such as an issue or a project. Relatable leaders will be aware of who the key decision makers are and decipher in what ways those decision makers could impact an outcome. By understanding the motivation behind hidden agendas, relatable leaders will be able to make more informed decisions for their team.

In addition to these conditions, individual behaviors act as a source of complexity. Even when leaders hire for attitude, complexities can materialize. Therefore, leaders need to be aware of three considerations in particular that can manifest within complex organizations:

1. The framing effect
2. The sunk cost effect
3. Resistance

With the framing effect, individuals have a skewed perception because of how something is presented to them and by whom. First introduced by Daniel Kahneman and Amos Tversky, two Israeli psychologists, the framing effect is a behavior that can hinder both leaders and their team. Leaders who are aware of the framing effect may alter the way in which they present options to their team to produce the desired results. Relatable leaders take into consideration how their team responds to direction from them and can reduce a negative outcome by using the framing effect to influence their team in a positive way. Additionally, relatable leaders should avoid the framing effect when individuals from their team approach them with new ideas. This deliberation allows leaders to make more informed and less biased choices.

The sunk cost effect is another human behavior that can add to the complexity of an organization. Rather than cut their losses and move on to a new project or initiative, sometimes people get stuck in the action of continuing down a losing path because they've already committed so much of their time and resources, emotions and energy, to that one failing project. Relatable leaders aware of the sunk cost effect should be able to identify when they are in a sunk cost situation. They also should trust their team to help them see when they've fallen into a sunk cost situation.

The third individual behavior is resistance. A person who refuses to embrace change falls into this behavior pattern. By not adapting to the changing environment, they are actually opposing the direction in which the leader wants to take the organization. Both leaders and team members can display resistance. Relatable leaders sensitive to resistance can remind themselves to be more open to change when other leaders propose new directions. They can also be more reflective in how they propose change to their teams. Therefore, those who are cognizant of the concept of resistance can alter the way in which they themselves react to change and the way they propose change to others.

Relatable leaders know how to identify these three behaviors, but what can happen when there's a whole group working against a leader's initiatives?

Group behavior can be categorized into three phenomena:

1. Groupthink
2. Groupshift
3. Self-organization

Be wary of groupthink. Groupthink is the abandonment of rational thinking as a result of the desire to conform to the group's collective mind, even if it's on the wrong path. It's an inhibiting factor that permeates through organizations and society and impacts a leader's ability to engage in value-based decision-making. Groupthink occurs because of faulty organizational culture and can occur at any level. As a result, organizational leaders should be aware of the underlying factors that guide employee behaviors toward groupthink. The most effective leaders have a comprehensive understanding of how groupthink can prevent teams from accomplishing their goals and how to avoid groupthink so teams work together to achieve their optimal performance.

To combat groupthink, leaders should reframe situations. It is essential that leaders perfect the process of reframing because it will help them approach problem-solving after examining a situation from multiple angles. For example, reframing allows leaders to determine the cause of a problem as seen by those involved in groupthink, as well as synthesize the cultural impact on the parties' decision-making and then incorporate this into the final solution. Thus, the solution to the problem can be architected through the prism of the additional frame of assessment, which will prevent the overarching cause of the initial problem.

Groupshift is the adoption of extreme positions that result in either risk-averse or risk-seeking behaviors. Self-organization is the act of several individuals banding together in sharp contrast to the established norms.

Two more behaviors leaders need to be cautious of, especially within senior management, are delusion and deception. Delusion is the act of executives falling victim to decision-making based on delusional optimism rather than on rational evaluation of existing options. Senior managers can tend to focus on unrealistic scenarios of success and overlook any potential miscalculations. I have seen this countless times, and perhaps you have seen this as well. So, what drives this behavior? One of the key drivers is the concept of inside view perspective. What I mean here is that executives make decisions on the assumption that the project or circumstance on hand represents a unique occurrence. As a result, they fail to consider other similar projects or circumstances when generating potential approaches to solving problems.

In addition to the inside view error, there are other factors to keep in mind. For example, executives engage in something called optimism bias and planning fallacy—the delusion that negative outcomes will not occur on "our" watch. Anchoring is yet another consequence of the delusion phenomenon. This bias occurs when executives lock their perception of assumptions and estimates based on poor information.

Deception is the other behavior leaders need to be cautious of. It is concerned with planning inaccuracies regarding politics and agency issues. One of the sources of deception is self-interest—the idea that executives make decisions that will help them, not necessarily help the overall organization. I'd also like to stress the variant risk preferences of leaders who may downplay certain risks to manipulate information and deceive the president or CEO in favor of their own agenda.

Finally, overoptimistic decision-making is another behavioral factor that increases an organization's complexity. Dan Lovallo, senior lecturer of management, and Daniel Kahneman, professor of psychology, discuss the following traits that lead to overoptimistic decision-making in their article "Delusions of Success: How Optimism Undermines Executives' Decisions."[2] Those traits are as follows:

* **Exaggerating personal talents.** Decision makers on projects often exaggerate their personal talents. They also tend to misperceive potential causes of events by taking credit for

unrelated positive occurrences and placing blame for negative outcomes on external factors.

* **Exaggerating their degree of control.** Decision makers tend to exaggerate the degree of control they have over specific events, rather than consider the role of chance.
* **Focusing on their own agenda.** Decision makers often focus on their own agenda while neglecting potential abilities and actions of rivals that could impact their organization's success.
* **Providing overoptimistic forecasts.** Due to the organizational pressures of multiple competing project initiatives, decision makers tend to provide overoptimistic forecasts in order to win approval.

Managing human behavior is not 100 percent achievable in any situation, and no discussion of human behavior is complete without examining emotions.

Leaders need to be aware of any potential situations that can trigger emotions. Intense emotions can cloud judgment and influence decisions, as I am sure you have either experienced or witnessed. Moreover, it is possible that emotions that surfaced because of one event will spill into the decision-making process of unrelated situations.

To combat such scenarios, leaders should familiarize themselves with the idea of emotional leadership. Leaders need to become aware of the impact of their own emotions and decisions on others. Taking this a step further, relatable leaders need to embark on a process of self-discovery that will help them adjust their leadership and management style to become in tune with others in the organization.

To help you succeed in your self-discovery and grow your emotional intelligence, psychologist and *New York Times* bestselling author Daniel Goleman[3] proposes a framework for emotional intelligence built on five components:

1. **Self-awareness**—The knowledge of personal emotions, strengths, weaknesses, values, and drivers and how they impact others. Self-aware leaders know how their feelings and actions are related, and they are aware of how their moods can influence the moods of those around them.
2. **Self-regulation**—The ability to control disruptive impulses and emotions. Leaders who are self-regulating also know how to manage conflict and take responsibility when their actions overpower others in a negative way.
3. **Motivation**—The intrinsic drive for achievement. Leaders who are intrinsically motivated have personal goals beyond external rewards.
4. **Empathy**—The consideration for the feelings of others during the decision-making process. Empathetic leaders know how to respond appropriately in emotional situations. I'd like to add here that beyond empathy, leaders should also have compassion. Compassionate leaders dive deeper by not only caring about the other person's feelings, but also about the other person holistically and understanding why the other person feels the way they do.
5. **Social skills**—The leveraging of relationships to direct people in the needed direction. Leaders with social skills are able to communicate effectively with others so they don't wonder about the leader's meaning and intentions.

Why is this framework relevant? As leaders, it's critical for you to understand your emotions and to be able to understand the emotions of those in your radius. By reflecting upon your emotional intelligence, you can begin to decipher how adept you are at understanding and managing your emotions and reacting to those emotions you recognize in others.

STAKEHOLDERS AND COMPLEXITY

Stakeholders are people operating within any one of your systems who have an interest or share in an undertaking or enterprise with you. Everyone you meet could be a stakeholder in your development as a leader, and those stakeholders could have a positive or negative impact on your endeavor. They could also have a direct or indirect impact on you, which is why it's important for you to know not just who your stakeholders are, but also how they will impact your life as a developing leader.

As with companies filling vacant positions within their organization, you'll have different stakeholders surrounding you at various stages of your development. As you get to know your strengths and preferences, you'll be able to see which stakeholders you want to invite closer into your life. Remember, you are the CEO of your life, so in the organization of your life, you want to surround yourself with others who support your growth. So, let's look at the power and influence of stakeholders.

Effectively managing your stakeholders ensures the best opportunities for your growth as a leader and for your overall success. Every stakeholder has a claim on your life in some way, and you want to make sure that anyone with a claim also wants what is best for you. Even though your stakeholders can affect your achievements, they are also affected by your achievements. For example, your spouse is a stakeholder in your life, and if you want to run for public office, your spouse, as a stakeholder, can help you achieve your goal and is also affected by you achieving that goal. Another example could be someone on your team. If you're a manager who wants to be promoted to a director, then your team reflects your ability to manage, and they will be affected by your promotion in different ways. Some people on your team might not get along with the new manager who replaces you, or someone from your team may be promoted to that manager role.

In a stakeholder study, project management professor Graham Winch[4] proposed several processes for stakeholder management, which are listed below. As you read his findings, consider how they relate to the people who have an impact on your life—personally and professionally.

* Identify stakeholders who have a claim on your life
* Categorize each stakeholder's claim
* Assess stakeholders' capacity to pursue their claims
* Manage the handling of any claims

Who are the stakeholders in your life? Now's a good time to take a moment and make a list of the people who have a claim on your life and who are interested in what you are doing. Keep in mind these people could be proponents or opponents. The proponents want you to succeed, and they might also benefit from your success. The opponents may be more adversarial, but they also have a stake in your success, whether they benefit directly or indirectly. Every stakeholder will come to your table with their own agenda and their own stakeholders in their own complex systems.

Once you have your list of stakeholders, categorize each stakeholder's claim on your life. Since my career is firmly grounded in project management, I find referencing project management concepts to be useful in my everyday life, and they apply here as well. In project management, stakeholder classifications could be

* internal or external to the company,
* ranked by project champions, project participants, community participants, or parasitic participants, and
* ranked by degrees of power and interest.

Internal stakeholders are your primary stakeholders. They are the closest to you, and they can supply you with something, demand something from you, or both. Examples of stakeholders could be your immediate supervisor and your child. Your immediate supervisor could supply you with development opportunities, which would help you become a better leader. Your child could supply you with a sense of compassion, which would also help you become a better leader. Both could also demand something from you, such as your time and energy.

In your workplace, your internal supply stakeholders are your consultants, contractors, and suppliers. Your internal demand stakeholders are your clients, sponsors, and financiers. External stakeholders are a bit more removed from your life, but they still have a claim on you. These include your neighbors or members of your team or employees within your department at work. They may want you to succeed, or they may be indifferent to your success, but they are still part of your system and can influence your life. In your workplace and in project management terms, the external stakeholders are grouped by private and public. The private stakeholders are residents, landowners, or environmentalists, whereas the public stakeholders are regulatory agencies or local and national governments.

Within these two stakeholder types, your stakeholders can be ranked as project champions, project participants, community participants, and parasitic participants. For example, your spouse may be an internal champion, whereas your child may be an internal participant. Community participants are essential to your sustained success as a leader. Parasitic participants have an indirect stake in your life, and they can be problematic because their focus is on how to promote their own personal gains, rather than how to support your growth.

In project management, project managers map the varying degrees of stakeholder interest and power. By creating a map that groups stakeholders in clusters of either proponents or opponents and then relating them to the project mission, and any specific problems and solutions that can occur on your projects, project managers are able to mitigate risk and reduce failure. Stakeholder mapping helps you as a leader visually determine who in your life has the highest level of interest and the highest level of power to help you achieve your goals. Winch argued that "one of the major differences between the failed project (TAURUS) and the successful project (CREST) was the effectiveness of stakeholder management."[5]

Figure 1 shows an adapted graph from Winch's TAURUS and CREST power interest matrices. These matrices were designed to categorize stakeholders based on who has the power to influence and who has a high level of interest. Essentially, Winch identifies those high on the power to influence and high on the level of interest scales as key players. While you may not be able to keep all your stakeholders happy at all times, by analyzing where your stakeholders fall within the adapted graph, you will have a visual representation of all your stakeholders.

FIGURE 1. Adapted Stakeholder Graph

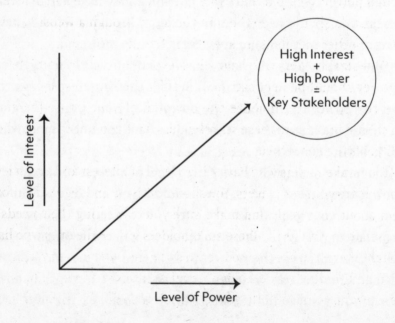

By using stakeholder mapping, you're able to adopt a strategy to manage your identified stakeholders. Based on the identification of each stakeholder along the power/interest matrix, you, as the CEO of your life, may classify your stakeholders as:

* requiring minimal effort,
* needing to be kept informed,
* needing to be kept satisfied, and
* being key players.

Once you have classified your stakeholders, you can customize how you interact with each of them. Your stakeholders who have a low level of interest and a low level of power require minimal effort. They won't expect you to spend too much time communicating with them, and checking in with them from time to time is sufficient to keep them as stakeholders.

Your stakeholders who have a high level of interest and a low level of power should be kept informed. These stakeholders might not have enough power to help or hurt you, but since they have a high level of interest, you should keep them in the loop through a website, newsletter, or other method(s) to keep them feeling informed.

Your stakeholders who have a low level of interest and a high level of power should be kept satisfied. Even if their interest is low, they have the power to influence the outcome of your goals. Therefore, you should make sure these stakeholders have their needs met where your goals are concerned.

Your stakeholders who have a high level of interest and a high level of power are your key players. You should actively and regularly inform them about your goals and make sure you're meeting their needs as they relate to your goals. These stakeholders will be the ones who have enough interest to use their power to sway the outcomes of your goals.

In addition to a stakeholder's level of interest and level of power to help you achieve your goals, Winch also notes the four main sources of relevant stakeholder power that can be applied to your leadership development:

1. **Positional power.** Relevant to a stakeholder's position in the organizational hierarchy.
2. **Resource power.** Relevant to a stakeholder's ability to provide resources.
3. **Expert power.** Relevant to a stakeholder's expertise and competence in a field.
4. **Personal power.** Relevant to a stakeholder's charisma to direct individuals' opinions.

After determining a stakeholder's power dimension, focus on adopting several strategies to manage the interests of each stakeholder. Again in Winch's article, we find some of these approaches (that we've abbreviated below) for the purpose of your own leadership development:

* **The alignment of incentives.** Ensure that stakeholders' incentives are aligned with your desired outcome.
* **Early development of a mitigation strategy.** Employ a consistent approach to handling any stakeholder claims.
* **Friends in the right places.** Have political allies to help manage external stakeholders.
* **An ethical approach.** Adhere to the corporate social responsibility of meeting and exceeding its obligations to stakeholders.
* **Getting the "concrete on the table."** Solidify stakeholders' support as early as possible as you forge ahead to complete your goals.
* **Strong public relations.** Keep external stakeholders informed about your progress without making them feel overwhelmed.

All leaders benefit from knowing who their stakeholders are in their personal and professional life. By learning how to communicate, build trust, and build interest in your own success, you can build multiple teams within your systems supported by stakeholders who will have a high level of interest in your success.

LEADERSHIP AND COMPLEXITY

Fresh out of graduate school, very early in my career, I learned that leadership and titles don't always align. As a project manager, I may be responsible for a project, but my team may be comprised of five or ten individuals from different departments. Therefore, I have no official authority over a person on the team who has a manager in a different department but who also reports to me for a project. The balance is tricky and can be stressful, and many people I've spoken with over the years can relate to this scenario—either reporting to two different managers or being asked to lead a team that they had no formal authority over.

Leadership is considered one of the most critical drivers for navigation of complexity on projects, and for the purpose of this book, I'll add that leadership is considered one of the most critical drivers for navigation of complexity in life. What is it about effective leaders that distinguishes them? Effective leaders nourish the lives of those around them, in particular their teams, by fostering human connection. This includes rewarding good work and offering emotional support and encouragement when the need arises.

In their book, *The Progress Principle*, business administration professor Teresa Amabile and developmental psychologist Steven Kramer propose four methods to help project leaders successfully nourish their employees. We've adapted these four methods to focus on leaders in general, not just project leaders. As you read through these methods, consider how they apply to the leaders in your life, to you as a leader, and to the many systems to which you belong—your family, coworkers, teams, and organizations.

Here are the four methods for nourishing you and those around you:

1. **Respect.** Treating yourself and your teams with respect shows that you recognize those around you as valuable contributors to your team and your life and helps build trust and commitment.
2. **Encouragement.** Being encouraging increases team members' beliefs in their own effectiveness and increases motivation.
3. **Emotional support.** Offering emotional support and compassion help strengthen connectedness on a team.
4. **Affiliation.** Cultivating a sense of affiliation encourages mutual respect and fosters the strengthening of bonds.

Nourishment is but one of the important leadership capabilities. In their article "In Praise of the Incomplete Leader," professors of management Deborah Ancona and Thomas W. Malone, professor of communication science Wanda J. Orlikowski, and leadership and sustainability senior lecturer Peter M. Senge[6] expand on the qualities of effective leaders by challenging each of us to reflect on four leadership capabilities and integrate them within our own mental model and experiences:

1. **Sensemaking.** Making sense of the world around us and how we operate within each of the complex systems that form every aspect of our lives.
2. **Relating.** Building trust, communicating and listening to your team's viewpoints, and cultivating supportive networks.

3. **Visioning.** Building commitment to growth through the sharing of a desired future.

4. **Inventing.** Providing innovative methods to address difficult problems while converting vision to reality.

In addition to organizing leadership capabilities, we need a method of organizing the complexity factors that affect the decisions we make as leaders. In their article "What a Difference a Word Makes," business professors Nathan Bennett and G. James Lemoine combine the factors into four distinct categories.[7] Because these categories can stall a leader's ability to plan and make predictions with any amount of certainty, leaders should have an appreciation for how these four categories influence their systems.

1. **Volatility.** Unstable changes that are frequent and unpredictable even though information may be available to help identify strategies. To address volatility, leaders need to employ strategies that can help them and their teams remain agile and flexible.

2. **Uncertainty.** While causes and effects are known, the impact of a change is unknown. Leaders need to employ creative ways to accumulate new information and approach potential problems from a variety of angles.

3. **Complexity.** The multiplicity of variables often creates a web of approaches and procedures that become complex to enforce. In this type of situation, leaders are encouraged to restructure the operations through effective and efficient methods in order to match environmental complexities.

4. **Ambiguity.** Where there is no available knowledge or pre-existing approach to address an existing scenario, leaders should consider experimenting intelligently to determine the most appropriate and beneficial strategies for the situation.

Leadership and being a leader are complex, but that doesn't mean it has to be complicated. In this chapter we covered a lot of information about the complexity of relatability. Relatable leaders are aware of the conditions that lead to complexity among humans and how individual and group behavior can manifest in their personal lives and within their professional organizations.

Relatable leaders are cognizant of how emotional intelligence can help strengthen their ability to manage their emotions and react to those emotions they recognize in others. This relates to the people who have an impact on their lives, their stakeholders. Classifying stakeholders allows relatable leaders to adopt several strategies to manage the interests of each stakeholder. By focusing on ways to nourish those around them, leaders become aware of the correlation between their leadership and the complex systems in their lives.

By arming yourself with the knowledge of how your many systems operate as complex adaptive systems, you become aware of situations and can reflect on ways to navigate their complexities. This navigation reflects on your relatability as a leader. The benefit of being relatable is the ease in which you function within the world, the largest system that you are a part of.

CHAPTER THREE REFLECTION

Leaders are part of many systems. Being aware of the complexities in our lives is one thing, but knowing how to move about, around, and address them successfully is something leaders continually need to work on. Fortunately, others have come before us and have taken the time to share what they've learned.

In this chapter's reflection, we'd like you to take a moment to consider all the ways you contribute to many complex adaptive systems. As a relatable leader, you position yourself within the hierarchy of systems with the realization that your behaviors and decisions affect all the systems of which you are a part, including yours and that of

- your family's,
- your colleagues' within a team or department,
- your colleagues' within the entire organization,
- teams', groups', or club members',
- your neighbors', and
- your community's.

Now choose one system and complete this phrase out loud or in the silence of your mind, and write it down:

My behaviors and decisions affect my systems in the following ways . . .

PART TWO
Think Outside the Box

When Simon and I were in our twenties, we entered the workforce where we wore business attire, had our own offices, and sat through countless meetings in conference rooms. As we moved within our organizations, our bosses asked us to think outside the box. They relied on our ability to critically assess a situation or an issue and devise a new approach. When someone asks you to think outside the box, what they're really asking is for you to take the knowledge you've acquired up to that point and add a new perspective. Your perspective will be unique to you since no one else will have lived in your skin. This is the time when we expand what we know. We use the new influences around us to create new ideas and broaden our definition of what it means to be a leader. In this section, we're going to ask you to think outside the box and find new ways to examine your life and your leadership development by exploring the five strategies relatable leaders use to cultivate their relatability: knowing their starting lines, increasing their cultural agility, practicing compassionate communication, embracing the leadership lifestyle, and viewing leadership as nonhierarchical. We're asking you to look at ways you can think outside the box, no matter where you started and what you already know.

4 Starting Lines

Many years ago, I taught high school students in a large county in Southwest Florida. In a county where the economic, demographic, and community profile report from the local government focused mainly on White and Hispanic as race options, I was sure my students were unfamiliar, if not uncomfortable, with a South Korean English teacher. After all, Asians made up less than 1 percent of the county's population. On the first day of school, many students entered the class, saw my eyes, and asked if they were in the right classroom—for English.

As the weeks progressed, the differences in the students' language arts skills and levels of comprehension shocked me. While reading one short story as a class, an Ivy League college was mentioned. One student asked what an Ivy League college was, and that was my first brush with the idea that not everyone in the ninth grade arrived with the same level of what I thought was general knowledge. As the lesson progressed, with an added discussion about college in general and what *Ivy League* means, I could see the student still was unable to grasp some of the concepts from the story. No matter how many different ways I tried to teach him, he wasn't learning. And it wasn't from his lack of trying. It was from my lack of experience. I couldn't teach the student because I couldn't connect with him on his level.

After thinking about this for several days, I devised an activity that went along with a journaling activity they were already doing, and I asked the students if they would do the journaling one day as an open class participation activity instead of a writing one. To my delight, all of them wanted to participate in this voluntary activity. For all my lessons, I included learning objectives, and for this one, the objectives tied into the short story we had read, where we explored characterization and points of view. By the end of the lesson, the students were able to critically think about how a character's perspective influenced their actions and opinions.

They all began the activity sitting down. If they had a two-parent household, they stood up. We agreed that having two parents at home was a good place to start, since both parents are mentioned in the beginning of the story. Then they came up with different advantages and disadvantages that had them either standing or sitting, followed by a robust discussion about our starting lines. It went something like this:

Mara, not her real name, lived in a house with two parents. She stood. Then she said one of the parents was her stepdad, and the class agreed that she should remain standing. But she shared a room with her sister, and they both had to walk to school because the family had only one car. The one car detail had everyone agreeing that she could sit down. Then she shared that she had her own room when she stayed with her biological dad. She stood. But she couldn't try out for cheerleading because she had to work after school. She sat. She also had to babysit her sister for free, and even though she had a cell phone, she didn't have her own computer. No one in her family had gone to college, and she didn't have plans to go either. She remained seated.

Jorge, not his real name, lived in a single-parent household. He remained seated. He shared that he worked an afterschool job, and he stayed seated. He had his own room with a desk and a laptop. He stood. He planned to go to a vocational school after high school, and he remained standing. At the end of the activity, it was interesting to note who was left standing and who was sitting.

This activity was based mostly on what the students felt were advantages and disadvantages in their lives. It helped us understand the perspectives of the characters in our future readings and each other. Even though *privilege* wasn't a buzzword back then, the concept of who was coming to the table with what experiences certainly helped me when providing feedback to those students. With the expansion of social media, I've since seen countless variations on this activity with the same intended lesson.

Teachers often say they learn from their students, and that exercise taught me that not everyone will have the same understanding of a situation because not everyone has the same starting line of knowledge. I hope they remember that activity when they're dealing with others who might not have access to the same advantages they did. For me, it was the first time I understood—as the teacher and adult in the classroom—the deeper need for compassion toward others.

We all have different starting lines, and in this chapter we're going to examine what that means by providing

* an introduction to positionality,
* an exploration of how intrapersonal communication impacts us,
* strategies for learning through experience, and
* a reflection upon your starting line.

POSITIONALITY

Positionality is the concept that a person's starting line forms the foundation upon which they view every facet of life and form opinions. It's the perspective from which a person understands the world.

We all have different starting lines. What's acceptable to you may be obnoxious to others. One person's way to show respect could be perceived by another as an insult. Your experiences help you make meaning of your life, and your circumstances define how you perceive others and the world around you. Positionality is informed by everything about you, including your gender, age, birth order, education, marital status, religious and political beliefs, socioeconomic status, and job titles or duties—everything that creates a reference point for how you view a circumstance. How you frame everything starts with your positionality.

Relatable leaders understand that each person's journey is unique, no matter where their starting line was positioned. They enter each interaction with two points of view in mind. First, relatable leaders recognize that their own point of view shapes their understanding of any interaction. Second, they recognize that the other person's point of view shapes that person's understanding of any interaction. This means that relatable leaders are able to interact with others without expectations beyond what they have learned from the other person.

THE PURPOSE OF UNDERSTANDING YOUR POSITIONALITY

As a child, you're a clean slate accumulating all these little experiences that become the norm for you. These norms form your behaviors. Understanding positionality and how it frames your experiences will help you gain a deeper perspective of yourself and develop an appreciation for other people's positionality.

There's a reason stereotypes exist, and that's because everyone makes assumptions based on their previous experiences. As you assess yourself as a leader and where you are now in your leadership development, it's important for you to recognize that this is not a neutral process. Everyone has personal biases and assumptions, all stemming from their personal and professional experiences. The purpose of understanding your starting line—your positionality—is to help you identify areas you can develop personally and devise ways to help others develop as leaders.

The thoughts we express, the language we use, and the topics we address all radiate our priorities and our voice. What we choose to display to the world classifies us by socioeconomic and cultural attributes and gender. The way we communicate reveals who we are and how we live our values. It begins to develop in childhood as we adjust and learn and grow. Over time, we pick up little things that become normal to us, and they form our worldview.

Some people say you only live once, and they're not wrong. But the philosophy we urge you to adopt on your journey to becoming a better leader is you only die once. You live every day.

Whether you've realized it before this moment or not, you are in charge of your life. You are the CEO, at the helm, making decisions every day, designing your present and your future. The first part of becoming a better version of yourself is knowing how your starting line shapes your actions and opinions, and that comes from understanding your positionality—your identity.

It wasn't until after I'd left the classroom that I came to understand my own journey, one that I think many experience in a similar way. During childhood, I was told to color inside the lines. In my twenties, I was asked to think outside the box by my bosses. In my thirties, after watching a rerun of *Ally McBeal* where I was first exposed to the you only die once philosophy, I reflected upon what I really wanted out of life. Simon and I had a lengthy discussion about what we thought we should be doing versus what we were doing versus what we wanted to be doing, and that's when we realized there is no box.

How does this relate to my positionality? I was adopted as a baby from South Korea. I saw myself as different from everyone else, and I desperately wanted to fit in. During childhood I would scold myself for smudging outside the lines. I would say I wasn't good enough. I would cry when a crayon wasn't sharp enough so I could color *just right*. Color with complete precision.

By my twenties, I'd spent so much time inside these self-imposed lines that I didn't know how to think outside the box. Yet supervisors and managers and many motivational speakers adopted the now common phrase *think outside the box*. Easier said than done. Especially if your starting line is in the center of a very large box, and that box is filled with stuff designed to weigh you down or keep you from even moving in any direction. What's outside the box? What more could there be? We didn't know what we didn't know.

During that lengthy discussion, with spreadsheets and lists of pros and cons, and an analysis of our college degrees and careers, Simon told me we didn't have to do what everyone else expected us to do. We could decide what would make us happy. It wasn't that simple, but that's how I remember it, and that's when I realized: I'd done this to myself—placed these limits and labels, positioned myself at the intersection of right here and almost there. I had boxed myself in.

So, I followed his advice.

He dared me to change our lives to ones filled with unlimited possibilities. Because of him, I leveled up in ways I never imagined. I asked myself *why not?* And then I promoted myself. I gave myself the title of CEO of my life. I gave myself permission to take charge of the direction of my life. And once I looked around me, really focused on what mattered most, the boundaries dissolved, and I saw there was never any box holding me back to begin with.

Still, being adopted, for me, means that not one person with my DNA wanted to keep me in their lives. It means that there will be times in my life when the burden will be on me to wade through the loneliness and hurt and anger that comes from having no one else like me to turn to in times when I feel so completely alone. It means that even if I turn to someone, that other person will never fully be able to understand what I'm going through and, really, how can I expect them to? It's not a mile in my shoes. It's a lifetime in my skin.

It's freeing to know that they don't get it. They don't have to because it's not their journey. It's mine.

As an emerging leader, it is up to you to find meaning and learn lessons from what you're experiencing. No other person is trying to become the person you are trying to become, just like no other person has had your experiences and your journey to get you to this point in your life.

Whether it's racism or socioeconomic difficulties, lack of parental support or a learning challenge, we all have something going on in our lives that creates roadblocks to leveling up. The first roadblock is you. It all comes back to you and how you allow yourself to react and learn and grow. Even someone with many advantages in life lacks the early experiences of facing certain obstacles that would provide a foundation for them to grow.

Learning is an ongoing process, and even if we were all preprogrammed to respond in a certain way, that doesn't mean we can't change our mode of thinking. In fact, if you google "change your thinking," millions of options load, offering advice on how to change your thinking and change your life. Even this book is designed to expand your worldview as you become your best self and your best self as a leader.

INTRAPERSONAL COMMUNICATION

Intrapersonal communication is the way we speak to ourselves. Our inner voice dictates messages to us with lightning-quick reflexes. This is why intrapersonal is the most important form of communication. You look in a mirror, and what does your brain tell you about how you look? It's your first thoughts every morning that reinforce your image of yourself. You might think to yourself that you look tired, that your hair is a mess or it's thinning or graying. You might check out the bags under your eyes or examine another wrinkle.

You go outside and it's raining. You tell yourself you're dumb for not grabbing an umbrella, you're stupid for choosing this slow lane in traffic, or you deserve a ruined outfit and being late to work because you're lazy or you're dumb or you're ugly or you're not good enough. You let yourself think these negative thoughts because this is your life. It's how it's always been—an unfortunate series of bad events surrounded by people prettier than you, smarter than you, in faster lanes than you're in. You start to make excuses for why they are where you want to be and you're not.

These negative messages your brain delivers affect how you send and receive messages with others around you. All the negativity that builds up inside you gets released in your attitude and your worldview. Several people, including writers Anaïs Nin and Stephen M. R. Covey, have been quoted as saying something along the lines that we see the world as we are, not as it is. And if we are negative, the world will seem negative.

If you're sitting there thinking, *yes, but that's not me. I'm not like that*, then that's fabulous! But do you know who is like that?

According to Fox News and the *Chicago Sun-Times* headlines, Americans are among the most negative people on Earth. This is reflected in the 2018 Gallup[1] survey:

* Americans are some of the most stressed people in the world.
* Nearly half (45 percent) of the people polled said they felt worried a lot of the time.
* More than one in five (22 percent) felt angry a lot.

The American Psychological Association has surveyed people about stress every year since 2007. In October of 2020, it reported that "3 in 5 (60 percent) say the number of issues America faces currently is overwhelming to them."[2] If that's not you, then it's probably someone on your team: a coworker, supervisor, manager, boss, or other employee. How do we change that? How do we shift our perspective from the negative to a more optimistic mindset? How do we push aside the anger, fear, and stress created by our circumstances to move forward? By understanding that each person's reality is how they interpret it, not how you do.

Relatable leaders use the knowledge of their own intrapersonal communication to identify with others around them. They want to support other people by spotlighting the benefits of having positive intrapersonal communication. This means, beyond building up others, relatable leaders stop others from putting themselves down. If your goal is to become a better leader, you need to be aware that there are people out there who are not having positive intrapersonal conversations with themselves.

From childhood, my starting line had deficits: abandoned as a baby, labeled a transracial adoptee, and raised by a widowed mother. I have issues because I'm not blonde, I'm not model thin, I'm . . . whatever it is that day. I have self-esteem issues, but I'm not alone. I think most people at some point experience impostor syndrome or self-doubt, and after shifting the way I speak to myself, I now understand what it takes to survive in this world where I'm standing at the intersection of being a female Asian adopted by white,

Catholic New Englanders. I also understand that at the core of every emotion we can find common ground with others experiencing that same emotion. That's why our intrapersonal communication is so important.

If that's not you, again, fabulous! I still encourage you to reference this book as a way to gain compassion for those who are likely experiencing these feelings.

Not everyone wants to be a leader, and not everyone should be a leader, but leadership can be found anywhere and in every facet of our lives. In every decision you make, you are leading yourself. Which is why it's so important to know yourself before you can figure out what type of leader you are or what type of leader you want to be.

When we begin to explore our own positionality, it is not neutral or apolitical. In order to produce a high-quality assessment of any leader, including yourself, it is necessary to recognize that your own subjectivity may hinder the credibility of your discovery. Your perspectives are limited to the constraints placed upon you by the perceived societal norms and the role models who raised you to understand them. Most agree that leadership has a relationship with influence, so look around you. Who are the individuals with the most influence upon your life? Who helped shape you and get you to where you are right now?

Your parents, teachers, and peers might be on your immediate list, and they might all have had conflicting messages at times. You are a mosaic of all the experiences you gathered as you grew to be the person you are today. These messages and how you choose to retain or forget them make up the foundation for your intrapersonal communication. That's the first piece of knowing your starting lines: reflecting upon the ways in which where you came from affects how you view yourself. Once you become aware of your starting lines, you can reflect upon who you are versus who you want to be.

WHO YOU WANT TO BE

One component of increasing your relatability is discovering how you make meaning of the experiences that helped you become a relatable leader. In their article "The Dawn of System Leadership" in the *Stanford Social Innovation Review*, cofounders of the Academy for Systemic Change Peter Senge and Hal Hamilton, along with Foundation Strategy Group board member and managing director John Kania state, "Good intentions are not enough. You need skills. But skills come only from practice. Everybody wants tools for systemic change. But too few are prepared to use the tools with the regularity and discipline needed to build their own and others' capabilities."[3]

Too often we've witnessed leaders saying the right things, but their actions didn't match their words. They didn't take the time to practice the skills needed to successfully commit to becoming a better leader. This spotlights the idea that you can teach leadership skills, but that doesn't correlate with those skills being learned and implemented in the right moment.

In 2019, president of Northeastern University Joseph E. Aoun remarked in his commencement speech that "Reinvention is how we truly progress. Reinvention requires agility, resilience, and creativity. Reinvention comes through experiences."[4] As you grow and change to become the leader you want to be, you'll go through versions of yourself to become your best leader self. Each time you face new situations, those new experiences will help you shift into another version of your leader self. As you build upon your starting line, we encourage you to seek new opportunities and new experiences that will add to who you want to be.

Reflecting back to that student and the Ivy League discussion, I more fully understand why I couldn't connect with him on his level. I lacked the experience needed to know how to reach him. Since that time, I've focused on experiences that help make me a better leader and help me connect with more people.

When deciding what kind of a leader you want to be and how you want other people to see you, you should be aware that leading is not one specific competency but a combination of attributes. Of course, this is what makes studying leadership so interesting to us, as replicable personalities lack authenticity. As you gain more experiences and allow those experiences to expand the way you view your life, the people in your life, and the world, you become better able to shift easily between the different roles you play in your life, and that ease becomes authentic to your personality.

LEARNING THROUGH EXPERIENCE

In 1984, David Kolb, credited with creating experiential learning theory, introduced the concept that "learning is a continuous process grounded in experience."[5] Further, he states that experience transforms into knowledge. This reveals the central role experience has on an individual's learning. You may have the prerequisites needed to become a leader, but how does someone actually learn to lead?

Essentially, experiential learning is learning by doing. The best way to learn something is to experience it, to reflect upon it by remembering the details of the experience, to think about what you've learned from it, and to act on what you've learned. That is why your starting line is the foundation upon which your learning is built. What you've learned up to this point and what you will learn in the future is grounded within your experiences. This experiential learning cycle happens whenever we encounter new experiences, demonstrating the limitless possibilities for us to learn and create knowledge. Relatable leaders seek out new experiences to help them become better leaders.

FIGURE 2. Kolb's Experiential Learning Cycle

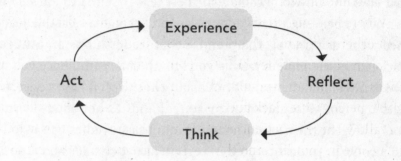

Becoming relatable is a process, and it takes time. It shouldn't be rushed because the experiences broadening your worldview shouldn't be rushed. You need time to be in the experience, think about the experience, reflect more deeply about the lessons learned from the experience, and act after having lived the experience.

For example, you attend a civic association luncheon. While there, you're in the experience. You meet with people, speak with them about various topics, listen to the keynote speaker, eat lunch, and maybe network a little before you leave. Later that evening, you think about the luncheon. Maybe someone asks you how it was or what happened or if you had a good time and learned anything new. You might replay the experience on the surface by recounting what happened. As you recall the luncheon, you also reflect upon the benefits of the experience and add an emotional connection to the memory. Did you see anyone sitting alone? Did you speak with anyone new? Were there any ideas presented that differed from your own? How did you feel about the keynote speaker's topic? Was there something you missed during the luncheon? How did you benefit from experiencing the luncheon? This deeper look into your experience allows you to form a new path for your next luncheon experience and change your actions.

While there is no one way to get to where you want to go, the most efficient way to become your best leader self is to enrich your life with experiences that help make you become a relatable leader. Since we're working off the premise that leadership is an influence relationship, the more relatable you are, the more influence you will have to a wider audience. It's not about checking off boxes of certain skills that you've acquired or mastered, and it's not about learning about different theories, although reading case studies can help you see how other leaders reacted in certain situations. It's about pursuing that which interests you in order to add more experiences to this one short and completely unpredictable life.

CHAPTER FOUR REFLECTION

In this chapter's reflection, we'd like you to intentionally take a moment to promote yourself to CEO of your life. Reflect on your positionality and how it relates to others with whom you interact. Draft a brief positionality statement that identifies your starting line, then think about how what you state compares with others in your social and work groups and with those who are the opposite or different from what you've stated here. Use the following questions as a guide:

- What is your age, race, ethnicity, gender, and birth order?
- Where did you grow up? Try to be as specific as possible.
- What is your social class, educational level, and health status?
- What careers did your parent(s) have and what were their educational levels?

- What other childhood factors influenced your personality? Did you go to church, Sunday school, summer school, or summer camp? Did you go on family vacations? Did you have two parents and multiple cars? At what age did you get a cell phone? Did you go to a private or public school?

This is you. This is your starting line. And everything about how you answered these questions could be analyzed to provide a snapshot of how you fit into the greater system of society. But just because you started here doesn't mean you have to stay here.

Now complete this phrase out loud or in the silence of your mind, and write it down:

In order to expand from my starting line, I need to include more experiences in my life, such as . . .

5 Cultural Agility

Many years ago, we attended an event at the Bulgarian Embassy in Washington, DC. After we left, we discussed many issues from the evening. The highlights included established leaders asking for our perspective on a topic, Bulgarians taking the time to speak to me in my first language of English even though it was clearly not their first language, and getting to meet others from different countries.

The fact that some diplomats and other leaders at the event asked us what we thought about different situations impressed on us that even though we were considered young at the time, our perspective added value to the conversation. It taught us to value the opinions of others, and we learned that knowledge can come from everywhere.

We saw compassion and kindness in those who spoke to me in English. They were able to shift into that mode for me to best relate to them, rather than making me feel uncomfortable and like an outsider. By meeting people from other countries, not just Bulgaria, and seeing how they interacted with us and with each other, we were able to get a glimpse of cultural agility in action. Furthermore, when people asked for my perspective as an Asian who grew up in America, they were increasing their own cultural agility.

The most relatable leaders use their knowledge of other cultures to understand how best to relate to other individuals. In this chapter, we're going to focus on the cultural agility of relatable leaders by providing

* a starting line for what cultural agility is and why it's important,
* a discussion about the power of being culturally agile,
* a definition for expansive inclusion, and
* a reflection upon your range of cultural agility.

THE IMPORTANCE OF CULTURAL AGILITY

Cultural agility helps leaders produce civil discourse and find common ground with people from different backgrounds. When relatable leaders understand the importance of cultural agility, they are able not only to be effective leaders to a broader range of people, but also to maintain authentic interactions with those people from cultures beyond their own. Relatable leaders assess the circumstances and shift their perspective to choose the best behavior to produce the most positive outcome, and they are able to take into consideration all the different ways people need leaders to care for them. They're able to do this authentically because they've developed a high level of cultural agility.

This cultural agility helps relatable leaders understand why someone from another country with a strict familial hierarchy in place might not be comfortable speaking up in the workplace unless spoken to first, and they use their cultural agility to know how to engage that team member. Being culturally agile also means relatable leaders are aware of social cues and can act in ways that won't offend others in a group. By making adjustments in their behavior, relatable leaders establish the mood in any given situation.

Within the last two decades, researchers have examined leadership from a cross-cultural perspective and focused on gender, race, ethnicity, and the intersectionality of race and gender. The Pew Research Center conducted a study in 2014 that showed political animosity among Americans is more polarized now than it had been during the last two decades.[1] With political parties focusing on issues as if they're black and white, compromise is no longer an expected solution. Rather, the two-party system elicits an either-or mentality and negates any middle ground, leaving little room for anyone who doesn't fit the party's ideology.

Despite the popularity of politically charged headlines in the United States media, global corporations erase boundaries and merge cultures. Multinational corporations hire more than 100,000 employees from around the globe, increasing the complexity of corporate culture and climate. Relatable leaders are culturally agile leaders. They understand how this interconnectedness impacts humanity globally and the challenge of finding common ground beyond the rising incivility among individuals. With more and more companies focusing on inclusion and diversity, marginalized groups are shifting the way humanity interacts and communicates with each other, and relatable leaders are vital in shaping an organization's culture.

Given the polarization of today's American society, *civil discourse* is a phrase that's creating fragmentation among many. Some people consider civility to equal silence, but that's not necessarily the case. Relatable leaders should be comfortable in situations where dissatisfied groups choose to voice their opinions. The Pew Charitable Trusts, Carnegie Foundation, National Association of Secretaries of State, National Alliance for Civic Education, and Center for Information and Research on Civic Learning and Engagement all understand the

importance of practicing civil discourse. CEOs of global conglomer-
ates must also understand the powerful role they play in shaping the
social world through written and oral discourse.

In the fall of 2016, more than 20 million students, where one in
four was a member of a minority group and approximately one million were international students, enrolled in more than 4 million
colleges and universities across the US.[2] This suggests civil discourse
could begin much earlier than during leadership development. It
could begin in college where students could learn how to communicate using language and behavior that promotes courtesy and
cooperation. This also spotlights the critical role of civil discourse as
students leave college and enter the workforce.

Relatable leaders are able to handle meaningful exchanges among
individuals with different starting lines. This is why we emphasize
the importance of experiences. As an emerging leader, you may not
know how to react in every situation, but relatable mentors and purposeful experiences will help provide a scaffolding for increasing
your cultural agility.

Most of our life is lived at the local level within our school districts
and voting districts, and this means our local communities have the
most impact on our daily lives. Even if you work for a Fortune 100
company and have plans to helm a multibillion dollar organization
one day, it will be the people in your daily life who will influence
and be influenced by your actions. That doesn't mean you shouldn't
expand your boundaries.

Throughout our early careers, Simon and I observed how leaders
in our everyday lives relied on their cultural agility to broaden their
range of influence in an ever-diversifying landscape. For example,
one of my first jobs was working for the business school at George
Mason University. The new director took the time to meet with me,
ask me about myself, and explain the objectives of the office where
I worked. Part of my duties involved presenting at information

sessions for potential MBA students. At first I observed the MBA applicants during their admission interviews, but later I took the lead during the interviews. Before leading my first interview, the director shared with me qualities I should look for in the candidates that went beyond the numbers presented in their undergraduate GPA and standardized GMAT scores. She shared with me the value in creating a cohort of students who represented a wide range of backgrounds and industry experiences.

Through this experience and the mentorship of my director, I witnessed how important it is to be able to interact with people from diverse backgrounds who have the same common goal—in this case being admitted to the MBA program. She also encouraged me to attend development trainings, even when the trainings took place during the workday. Through my director's mentorship, I was able to feel the power of being culturally agile. As I conducted more interviews with people from diverse backgrounds, I became more comfortable interacting with them, thus increasing my own cultural agility.

By focusing on creating a diverse student cohort, my director also increased her range of influence by reaching a wider audience from many different backgrounds and industries within the community. Most of the applicants had between two and ten years of work experience, and we were able to connect with individuals employed in the public and private sectors, within nonprofits and government, and across large and small industries such as construction, finance, food, and technology.

Recently, Simon and I read an article by organizational psychology experts Kyle Lundby and Paula Caligiuri. They devised a cultural agility climate measure that really caught our attention. Their survey examines the perception of global competitiveness in relation to leaders, managers, coworkers, tools, and resources, and it outlines the critical factors necessary to address when creating culturally agile leaders. As they point out, "We don't just need agile leaders, we need everyone—from top to bottom—to be aware of differences and able to operate effectively in a global environment—even if they never leave the United States."[3] This study confirmed the role of leaders and their influence through communicating with their organizations.

But where does increasing your cultural agility begin?

In many real-life situations, we will find ourselves working within diverse teams. Diversity can be measured by the degree of similarities and differences among members of the team. This may include gender, age, ethnicity, socioeconomic backgrounds, educational levels, and other factors, such as areas of expertise. Instead of closing off from others who are different from them, relatable leaders seek ways to expand their circle of people in ways that enhance their cultural agility.

However, cultural agility takes practice. People who are first exposed to a new or unfamiliar culture may experience culture shock when they find that others do not abide by the same social norms as they do. The more our society shifts toward inclusion, the more defensive some people can be toward others who differ from their own default settings. We have met some closed-minded leaders who used their power to get what they needed from people. We hope that as companies utilize the digital landscape to expand, they also make space for their team to learn how to embrace cross-cultural experiences.

Fortunately, previous researchers have illustrated the critical importance for leaders to be able to shift among and within multiple cultural contexts and how applying this competency is vital for crafting a leadership lifestyle. Culturally agile leaders know how to interact authentically in cross-cultural situations and with all members in their professional and personal lives. As leaders, we must learn to be culturally agile. We might not be male or female, from New England or South Korea, but we might work with people from places we are not from. We might be on a team with someone who was raised in a different socioeconomic bracket than we were, and we might be asked to collaborate with someone who has never been to the country we were raised in.

Who a person is shapes how that person perceives the world. Relatable leaders recognize how their own subjectivity controls their perspectives, and that their perspectives are limited to the constraints placed upon them by perceived societal norms and the role models who raised them to understand these norms.

A leader's positionality and level of cultural agility inform and limit their ability to make an impact on the people in their lives. Whether they realize it or not, leaders of our global organizations have the ability to impose their beliefs and values on their employees, their customers, and even other organizations that encounter them. Industry titans create the spectrum of right and wrong. As emerging leaders, it is your challenge to observe the people around you and assess their behavior. As leaders, you hold an enormous responsibility. People use leaders as a frame of reference for how to operate within society, function within a community, and choose the next leaders. Existing leaders have power in deciding who gets seen and who remains invisible.

THE POWER OF BEING CULTURALLY AGILE

People use a variety of styles to communicate, and the way we express ourselves affects how others perceive us. Depending on our word choices, the topics we initiate, and the conversations we participate in, others will make assumptions about us, such as what our gender or ethnicity is. As global corporations continue to hire employees from around the world, individual cultures are merging with organizational ones. Adults already in the workforce are learning to adapt to cross-cultural engagements, but without the proper education or training to promote cultural adaptability, efforts to produce positive corporate results may fail.

Organizations

Leadership is essential for the success of any organization. Without it, companies would not meet their objectives to deliver products and services to their customers. Organizations are no longer confined to one local area, and many businesses are unable to operate without the use of technology, which widens the digital landscape across cultures and time zones. Multinational corporations hire employees from around the globe, increasing the complexity of corporate culture and climate. The racial and ethnic diversity promotes active thinking skills and intellectual engagement. The challenge facing organizations is finding common ground beyond the rising incivility among individuals. As these organizations continue to hire employees from around the world, individual cultures merge with organizational ones.

Since cultural agility helps leaders produce civil discourse and find common ground, organizations benefit from hiring and developing relatable leaders. Relatable leaders understand the importance of cross-cultural communication in global organizations, and they welcome collaboration with people from other backgrounds, cultures, and viewpoints. Culturally agile leaders are able to seamlessly shift into each situation and effectively lead diverse groups with multiple perspectives.

Culturally diverse teams may find it challenging to achieve open communication. This lack of communication can hinder a team's creativity and its ability to be productive. Overall, diversity among teams and organizations with culturally agile members and leaders are better able to meet the global challenges facing today's organizations.

In order to examine how culturally diverse teams can achieve open communication, professors Christian Troster, Ajay Mehra, and Daan van Knippenberg conducted a longitudinal study using data from ninety-one self-managed teams comprised of 456 individuals representing sixty nationalities.[4] The study examined the effects of a team's workflow structure and its cultural diversity on the team's confidence in its ability to perform. The study also examined the team's performance as rated by expert judges.

Two team challenges found in the study were interpersonal conflict and lower levels of coordination. The team's performance was interactively shaped by the structural characteristics of the team and the diversity of team members, where diversity for this study focused on nationality in terms of different countries and the different ideas and beliefs stemming from those countries. A team's performance can be assessed not only in terms of how well it actually performs, but also in terms of how confident its members are that it will go on to perform well. Diverse teams also bring different ways of thinking, and ambiguity about one's role within a team can hinder peak performance within that team. When the workflow and goals are clear, misunderstandings decrease, and everyone's confidence in completing their assigned roles rises.

Relatable leaders recognize their responsibility to be sensitive to potential ambiguity and to clarify every team member's role, as well as to articulate each person's value to the group. By supporting culturally agile leaders and their employees, organizations organically create holistic leaders beyond the traditional competencies to include networks and relationships. Culturally agile teams learn to respect cultural differences and capitalize on how best to use those differences to create the best possible solutions for their organizations.

Education

Effective leaders are found throughout an organization, not just at the top, and organizations are dedicating significant amounts of time and money to develop and train emerging leaders in their organizations. When leadership is viewed as a process of influence, it can be executed by individuals throughout an organization. Because most companies, both small and large, do business online and gain exposure through social media, they must focus resources on training emerging leaders in a combination of technical, conceptual, and human skills. Leadership development programs are the perfect place to cultivate emerging leaders' cultural knowledge and reflection skills after experiential learning takes place.

Donna Rich Kaplowitz, teacher education professor; Jasmine A. Lee, scholar-practitioner and activist; and Sheri L. Seyka, high school English chair, examined the way college students engage high school students in learning about racial identity and difference.[5] They note that "80% of public school teachers are white but almost half of students are not." They point out that without the willingness and knowledge of how to engage in racial conversations, educators will not be able to model how civil discourse could help bridge boundaries.

The intergroup dialogue methodology merges two or more social identity groups in facilitated race and culture conversations. In the study involving thirty universities, intergroup empathy and understanding of race, gender, and income inequality increased. Both quantitative and qualitative responses reveal that both the college student discussion leaders and the high school students increased their ability to critically think and actively listen to racial issues.

In order to help college students realize the impact of their opinions, communications professors Darren L. Linvill and Andrew S. Pyle created an inquiry-based civil discourse education activity with three main objectives: "(1) increase their capacity to examine arguments critically, (2) enhance their own ability to self-reflect critically, and (3) improve their ability to engage in civil discourse."[6] Not only does the activity expose students to uncomfortable topics and challenge opinions, but it also helps them find value in their role in civil discourse.

If you are not immediately in contact with culturally diverse teams, how do you learn about different cultures? After all, developing cross-cultural competencies improves your reach and effectiveness as a relatable leader, and there is plenty of research that supports the idea that experiential cross-cultural exercises among individuals from different cultures and countries help ease uncomfortable conversations and leave people better able to navigate and lead cross-cultural teams.

People become more culturally agile when they seek to acquire knowledge beyond their own assumptions, and leaders who learn to be culturally agile exceed the demands of the growing economy. As you continue to create experiences toward becoming a relatable leader, choose encounters that will broaden your own viewpoints. Gaining cultural competence happens over time, and the more experiences you have and reflect upon, the better able you'll be to relate and be relatable.

Digital and Media Landscape

One of the most telling indicators of why cultural agility is so important is the way America is portrayed through television documentaries. In an analysis of public television from 2007 to 2016, a team of researchers conducted a quantitative content analysis, examining the geographic, demographic, and topical diversity between television documentaries and the US Census and polling data. The research questions related to who makes the films, where in America the filming spotlights, whose stories are being told, and what social issues are being focused on. Findings from the data conclude that Independent Television Service–funded filmmakers produce films reflecting the diversity of lives and people in contemporary American life from all quadrants of the United States, including both rural and urban communities. In other words, based on the results from the study, the Independent Television Service–funded films are revealing a portrayal of a diverse America and contributing to the conversation by showcasing "the lives, concerns, and experiences of a geographically, racially, and ethnically diverse group of Americans."[7]

Within the investigation of communication within the digital landscape, anthropology professor Neha Vora examined the topics of belonging, freedom of speech, and rights through the United Arab Emirates blogosphere as part of a larger ethnographic research project. Citizens and noncitizens interacted online, and assumptions were made among citizens, expatriates, and migrants. In one post, Vora notes a male expatriate community moderator informing a female Emirati citizen "that she is no longer welcome in the community."[8] This was in response to the female Emirati citizen expressing what the male expatriate perceived to be criticism against the state.

Though the site is an English-language community, Vora notes the difference in belonging and participation between Westerners and Middle Easterners. Westerners are allowed to criticize the state, whereas Middle Easterners are not. It is of interest to note that in the case of the United Arab Emirates English-language blogs, "Muslim and Arab citizens emerge as marked subjects who test the limits of a transnational public through their supposed inability to be civil in civil society."[9] This leads into the role discourse plays within the public and the media, and the critical need for relatable leaders who understand the benefits of being culturally agile.

America is more diverse than ever before, and with the globalization of corporations and the expansion of the internet, humanity is interconnected in ways beyond geography. By embracing diversity and taking note of what we watch on television and who is seen in those programs and commercials, we can begin to increase our relatability by expanding our frame of reference.

Communications professors Kent A. Ono and Ronald L. Jackson II reference numerous environmental, economic, political, and social issues confronting humanity:

> The 9/11 attacks on the World Trade Center, wars in Iraq and Afghanistan, tsunamis in Asia, Hurricane Katrina, genocide in Darfur, the global economic crisis, driving while black and brown, the earthquake in Haiti, floods in Pakistan, the burgeoning prison industrial complex, the repeal and reinstatement of the "Don't Ask Don't Tell" policy, disappeared women in Juarez, Mexico, and tensions between North and South Korea.[10]

These happenings spotlight the relevance of an increased effort toward civil discourse within the field of communication. Given the digital landscape, as well as media interactions, Ono and Jackson remark upon four scholars' essays relating to civic and civil discourse. The first essay points to the lack of public values as a social problem. The second essay focuses on space for civil conversation within the newspaper op-ed. The third essay examines the way media uses pity versus genuine empathy to comment on power relations between subjects. The fourth essay reflects not only on US perceptions in regard to race and immigration, but also on perceptions of self. All four scholars acknowledge the need for civil discourse in the face of complex social issues that cross cultures and enter the digital landscape.

Relatable leaders view media open-mindedly and critically so they can consider the source, point of view, and even the verbiage of the content. One activity you can do to help expand your awareness is to use an alternate point of view to rewrite some of the headlines you see. This will help increase your compassion and broaden your range of acceptance.

Here's a simple example: Homeless Man Beaten after Stealing Bread.

As is, the first instinct of a person reading this headline might be to feel bad for the guy, but it also might be to think the neighborhood is declining or that a man experiencing homelessness is a thief. But as an emerging leader, we'd like you to consider for a moment how that title could be rephrased.

Why was the man stealing bread? The obvious answer is that he was hungry and wanted to eat. Imagine how desperate that man must have felt to commit an illegal act for bread. Not for a filet mignon or a bottle of Cristal, but for bread.

Now, and perhaps more importantly, who beat this man? Unless it was another homeless man, we can assume that the person who beat the man was the stronger of the two—meaning fed, clothed, and sheltered. Does this change in perspective make you see this as a bit like the king kicking the kitten? How could you rewrite the headline to change how a person perceives the article? We're not journalists, but here are two examples to flip the script:

1. Store Owner Beats Starving Man Experiencing Homelessness
2. Store Owner Stops Starving Man Who Stole Bread

This puts the store owner as the subject acting in the story. In the two examples, the headline starts with the person of privilege acting upon someone who has less privilege. Without knowing anything about the homeless man, his reasons for being homeless, or why theft was his action of choice, you've hopefully felt a bit of compassion for the hungry man and a tug inside you for a call to action. Whether this was the first time or the tenth time the store owner lost money because someone stole from them, by reframing the headline, you're able to engage your cultural agility by considering both sides in the situation. By reflecting on the situation, you can show you care by asking yourself how you can help eradicate hunger, if not also homelessness.

This is an example of how positionality and power are interconnected. Because your positionality is informed by everything that shapes your perspective, your power in this situation comes from two places: your ability to engage your cultural agility and your ability to influence change. Your positionality also reveals how much power you have to act upon a problem, in this case hunger or homelessness or store security.

We don't know the store owner's positionality, but we can make an assumption that the store owner has enough food. It was within the store owner's power to handle the situation differently—nonviolently. Even if the store owner was deep in debt and unable to afford to give the man any food, the store owner still entered the encounter from a position of privilege and power over the hungry man experiencing homelessness.

We realize the media will continue to produce headlines that may or may not frame racism, sexism, or other marginalized people in an accurate light. But if you do this exercise a couple of times a day for the rest of your life, you will continue to cultivate your relatability by increasing your cultural agility.

Politics

Regarding leadership and education, Robert R. Alford and Harry M. Scoble studied political involvement and education, finding that leaders—governmental or otherwise—were most frequently drawn from those with the highest education, occupational status, or income.[11] This means that public servants start with a particular amount of privilege, being at least middle class, and need to cultivate their relatability and cultural agility to most effectively represent all their constituents. Emerging leaders who wish to run for office or become involved in community leadership in some way would benefit by adding experiences to their lists that provide them additional perspectives and allow them the opportunity to practice civility through mutual respect and mutual understanding. Relatable leaders proactively communicate with others and share their knowledge with others from diverse groups.

According to Microsoft researchers Elad Yom-Tov, Susan Dumais, and Qi Guo, "Exposure to differing viewpoints has been shown to be socially advantageous in several ways;" however, extant literature indicates that "people tend to read political opinions that agree with their own opinions."[12]

The researchers examined whether civil discourse could be improved by increasing an individual's exposure to varied political opinions through the use of web services such as news aggregators and search engines. While testing the possibility of encouraging people to read opposing views, it was discovered that people become more interested in the news when exposed to more than one view on a topic. People who continued to read opinions similar to their own also read opposing opinions when the language closely resembled their own language.

Similar to the reframing of headlines exercise mentioned in the last section, relatable leaders seek opportunities to read opposing views, and by doing so, create a deeper well of knowledge from which to form their opinions and make decisions.

EXPANSIVE INCLUSION

Leaders will always have an instinctual way to react to a situation, but relatable leaders push outside their comfort zone by tapping into their cross-cultural knowledge and relying on their experiences before instinctually reacting. Almost a decade ago we participated in a conversation with community leaders discussing what support to add for marginalized groups, and as one of the proposed solutions, we flipped the conversation to inquire about what obstacles could be removed. Many barriers exist for marginalized groups, particularly in education and leadership development as they enter the workforce. Instead of giving them a box to climb over the fence, sometimes we achieve the same goals by removing the fence.

A teacher once said you shouldn't be nice to your students because the world won't be nice, and it's bad to set them up for failure. I've asked why wouldn't the world be nice to them, and isn't treating them the same as everybody else setting them up for failure? If we instead do things to support their success so they can feel what it's like to succeed, they then will likely help other people succeed. If enough people learn this, then more and more barriers to success will be removed for more people.

In considering our own definitions of leadership, role models, and responsibilities as leaders, we found ourselves challenging what we were raised to think, how we had witnessed leadership in the past, and what we considered to be genuine inclusion. Relatable leaders promote cultural awareness by engaging in expansive inclusivity.

DEFINING EXPANSIVE INCLUSION

Maria Morukian, professional certified coach and intercultural communication expert, states that "Expansion is building community across the landscape of our differences. Expansion requires us to explore beyond the comfortable social networks in which we typically reside, where we not only tolerate but actually seek out divergent voices and perspectives, and constantly challenge our own ideologies."[13]

A LEARNED COMPETENCY

As a teacher, I learned that each and every student learns in ways unique to them. In order for me to be able to reach the most students, I needed to be able to teach them more than just a single concept and teach them in a way that they could learn. The way I instinctively taught was not necessarily the way they instinctively learned. As a result, I had to learn hundreds of ways to teach because a relatable leader knows hundreds of ways to lead.

One of the most culturally agile leaders I've worked with is Nicole Resciniti, president of The Seymour Agency. She displays a unique ability to seemingly effortlessly shift into any situation and effectively communicate with anyone. Whether the environment is new or familiar, Nicole draws on her previous experiences to adapt to the circumstance. One observation we've made over the years is that this competency was learned as she gained more experience in multiple situations. Through her travels internationally, she was exposed to different cultures and embraced the context of each country she visited. Because she's the president of a literary agency, she also works with people from all over the globe who work in a variety of professions. From foreign rights agents to audio and film producers, and across a wide range of nonfiction specialties, Nicole has learned how to relate to others in a way that allows those around her to feel comfortable and connect with her.

That is the power of a culturally agile leader.

WHAT BEING CULTURALLY AGILE MEANS

Most researchers who study and report on diversity agree that diversity within organizations that have culturally agile leaders creates culturally agile employees who are better able to position themselves and their organizations within a global landscape.

Today's leaders face domestic and foreign challenges, and another layer of complexity is added when teams are formed virtually to connect employees across multiple countries. Online software helps leaders bring their teams together, but everyone still needs to be mindful of the differences in time zones, holidays, and cultural norms that are not standardized across continents. Even when teams are located in a central place, individuals who lack cultural agility could still experience challenges with how they communicate with their coworkers. With the right kind of diversity and inclusion efforts, everyone will feel like they are respected and supported regardless of their ethnicity, age, religion, gender, or other distinction.

Relatable leaders accept the challenge of operating with cross-culturally populated organizations. When relatable leaders collaborate with each other, they are able to influence change and create a positive sustainable organizational culture, but finding common ground is essential to organizational communication. Even with seemingly increased fragmentation, there needs to be productive discussions toward equitable solutions. Relatable leaders continue to engage in civil discourse because they understand how today's interconnectedness impacts humanity globally.

In this digital age, people are able to connect with a wider range of cultures throughout the world, and relatable leaders take advantage of this opportunity to increase their cultural agility and expand their range of influence. A global economy means a more complex networking system. Advancements in technology mean more awareness about politics and foreign issues, and relatable leaders continually develop their competencies to handle the challenges facing cross-cultural teams. When team members form an understanding of each other's capabilities, it results in improved coordination of their actions.

Since cross-cultural exercises prove successful in increasing cultural intelligence, you might consider adding ways to increase your interaction with people of all ages from different cultures and countries. By working on ways to recognize and support expansive inclusivity, you'll have opportunities to not only respect the rights of others, but also reflect a concern for justice for all. Because learning is a continual process, relatable leaders use leadership development to share perspectives on relevant issues and work toward solutions in the public interest. By understanding the importance of becoming culturally agile individuals, leaders are better able to understand how to communicate civilly with each other.

CHAPTER FIVE REFLECTION

In this chapter's reflection, we'd like you to take a moment and think about the people in your life with whom you interact on a daily or weekly basis. Culturally agile leaders are self-aware and use their own biases to develop their immunity to cultural stereotyping. By answering the following questions, you will be able to assess your cultural agility and see how limiting or how expansive your exposure to other cultures is.

- How old were you when you had a teacher in school who was not the same gender, race, or ethnicity as you?
- How many people who are not your gender, race, or ethnicity do you interact with on a daily or weekly basis? In what capacity do you interact with these people?
- In a professional capacity, do you work with people who are not your gender, race, or ethnicity? Are they your boss, colleague, or subordinate? Do you have beliefs and biases that contradict your boss's, colleagues', or subordinates'? In what ways?

Cultural Agility

Your responses will help you see if there are areas of your life where you are missing opportunities to organically increase your cultural agility.

Now complete this phrase out loud or in the silence of your mind, and write it down:

Experiences that will help me increase my cultural agility include . . .

6 Compassionate Communication

In his book *Outliers, New York Times* bestselling author Malcolm Gladwell states, "The kinds of errors that cause plane crashes are invariably errors of teamwork and communication."[1] Gladwell gives the example of Avianca Flight 052. As summarized by Gladwell, the captain repeatedly asked for directions from air traffic control to be translated and to be repeated louder. The first officer on the plane remained passive in the face of their emergency. Instead of reporting that they did not have enough fuel to continue flying in a holding pattern before landing, they said they were running low on fuel, which, as Gladwell points out, is common for all planes at the end of a flight. But it wasn't only what was said, it was how it was said. Gladwell quotes one of the controllers who said, "There was no urgency in the voice."[2]

In certain situations, mitigated speech shows politeness or a deference to authority. Hierarchies in certain cultures are clearly established, and in today's digital landscape and global economy, we interact with the most diverse population ever, socioeconomically and ethnically.

Communication isn't part of the game; communication is the game. But we can't communicate what we don't know, and communicating effectively starts with compassion. In any situation. In any group. Relatable leaders recognize the value of compassion. They are able to have meaningful conversations by entering each exchange with a caring attitude that values the other person. When communication lacks compassion, cues can be misunderstood or misread.

Relatable leaders stand at the intersection of hope, possibility, and reality, and they seek solutions for the whole picture. In this chapter, we're going to focus on compassionate communication by providing

* a discussion of the importance of compassion,
* a discussion of how individuals grow through compassionate communication,
* examples of how culture and communication intersect,
* a discussion of how ethics correlates with the ways in which leaders use compassionate communication,
* a discussion of the ways in which leadership is a choice, and
* a reflection upon your communication style.

THE IMPORTANCE OF COMPASSION

Empathy occurs when someone experiences another person's emotions as if the emotions were their own. Not everyone can feel what someone else feels. Not everyone is an empath. Compassion occurs when someone understands another person's distress and wants to help them find solutions. Once I understood the difference, I realized that compassion can be taught and learned, and I decided that I'd rather be part of the solution than criticize the problem.

While it would be nice for everyone to feel empathy, leaders with compassion are taking their responsibility as a leader one step further. Compassionate leaders seek not just to understand and be sensitive to their team, but also to look for ways to help everyone, even those not on their team. Compassionate leaders understand, are sensitive to, and respect their team members' feelings and views. Team morale tends to be high under these circumstances.

For a while I had empathy, but I didn't have compassion. I could empathize with those close to me and around me, and I could make the effort to place myself in their shoes, but what that did was limit my viewpoint to theirs. By attempting to see the situation through their perspective, I shut off my own way of perceiving the issue. As a leader, I wanted to find that space where I could move beyond emotion and act on the feeling.

The lesson I learned when I purposely chose to focus on compassion over empathy was that I no longer felt bound to the emotions of my team. I could empathize, but I could also act, and by choosing to act on that emotion, I was tapping into compassion. After all, if two people on my team have a disagreement, it would be impossible for me to fully empathize with one if I'm truly empathizing with the other. Compassion allows me to act and help everyone move toward a resolution.

This mindfulness can be learned through placing ourselves in situations where we, as leaders, ask ourselves how we can help someone else.

GROWTH THROUGH COMPASSIONATE COMMUNICATION

Many people in the workforce are asked to think outside the box. Outside the box implies there's an inside the box, and as we explored in the first part of this book, inside the box is related to what we have learned that has helped us form our perspectives. Our personal values drive behavior.

The theory of planned behavior suggests that individuals will engage in a given behavior when attitudes toward such behavior are most favorable. Since attitude is the mode through which individuals express their beliefs, we can see why values influence resistance to change. For example, an employee had been with my organization for over two decades. During her tenure, she witnessed many coworkers losing favor with senior management after they openly spoke against certain initiatives. Subsequently, many of them lost their jobs. As a result, this coworker adopted a belief that speaking up would have a negative effect on her career, so she refrained from sharing her thoughts about any proposed changes for fear of losing her job. This adaptation required a modification of her personal values regarding openness, learning, and even justice.

When she landed on my team, I proposed that employees should speak their minds openly during staff meetings, but this employee resisted on the basis of her altered values. She offered several reasons, including that old ways have worked, so why change now; new ways will take too much time to learn and will cost money; her friend told her this was tried before in another company and it failed; and she hates any changes proposed by certain individuals, because she mistrusts those individuals.

To address many of these types of resistances, I employed several principles. The most successful was having leaders diagnose the stakeholders who hold their values most firmly and devise a strategy that could help win over these stakeholders. This principle was successful because loyalties in the organization play a key role in swaying the popular vote, and such loyalties are based on hidden alliances built over the long term among many employees. Failing to recognize such alliances and devising a plan to win them over can result in collective resistance.

I explored the situation further to see if there were any other employees who behaved similarly. During staff meetings, everyone was encouraged to speak their minds. When no one did, I decided to investigate further to determine if this was a collective problem. I scheduled interviews with senior management about prior leadership and whether there had been specific penalties for employees who spoke up openly.

Next, I set up a box for people to submit anonymous notes about changes that needed to take place. The box was in a discrete place, away from cameras and open areas so that no one could see who deposited the notes. I reviewed the notes and found evidence of existing problems. This supported my theory that there was an agency-wide issue. I needed to implement strategies to encourage open communication. So we established special incentives for people to speak up, role-played during staff meetings to get everyone involved and talking, had after-work happy hours to build informal communication practices, and played team games.

Some additional issues transpired with the employee, and I had a private conversation with her to let her know that I had appointed her to be my special adviser. With over two decades of experience, she would be an extremely valuable subject matter expert, and I gave her more control over specific decisions. I also provided her with special incentives and offered her encouragement or moral support when she shared an opinion openly in front of the rest of the staff. As a result, her behavior changed over time.

But before I had done all that, I had to figure out a way to relate to her. Then I had to use compassionate communication to show her that I understood how she felt and make her feel seen. This approach would not have been successful without thinking outside the box of what had been done in the past or without encouraging others to challenge what had become the norms of communication in the organization.

CULTURE AND COMMUNICATION

Researchers have noted that a reason multicultural teams are prone to experience more conflicts than teams whose members all share a similar culture is that the differences in cultural values affect how team members communicate. In a TEDxMaastricht talk, leadership expert Simon Sinek says, "The very survival of the human race depends on our ability to surround ourselves with people who believe what we believe. When we're surrounded by people who believe what we believe, something remarkable happens. Trust emerges . . . Trust comes from a sense of common values and beliefs."[3] He then goes on to share an example using our children as the most valuable possession on the planet:

You want to go out on a date and require a babysitter. You have two options: a sixteen-year-old within the community with little or no babysitting experience or a thirty-two-year-old who just moved into the neighborhood with ten years of babysitting experience. In his example, Sinek posits that you would rather choose someone within your community with no experience over someone you don't know but who has a decade of experience.

This is a magnificent example of how we prefer to do business with people like us and trust people like us over strangers despite their qualifications. It's perfect, really, and we challenge anyone who disagrees with this premise. But if trust comes from a sense of common values and beliefs, how do we trust people from other backgrounds and cultures? How do we become more comfortable with others who believe in something different from what we believe?

Let's take the television show *House* as an example. In this show, a doctor specializing in diagnostic medicine tackles the toughest or most interesting cases, and he does this with a diverse team. Plenty of research exists as to why diversity in health care should be a must-have and not just a nice-to-have. Diversity on a diagnostic team—or any team—widens the team member's vision and allows them to look at problems from multiple perspectives. The more diversity, including a range of ages, backgrounds, beliefs, and ethnicities, the wider that vision can get.

But not every diverse team works well together, and instead of team members pushing each other forward, they get stuck. Forward momentum happens when the team members know how to communicate with compassion. When we think about all the reasons we might not be comfortable with someone who has a different starting line, some—if not many—of those reasons stem from our miscommunications or lack of knowledge.

Relatable leaders use compassionate communication to find ways to trust people who might hold different beliefs. They cultivate their relatability by increasing their cultural agility so as to become more comfortable with other cultures and backgrounds and not allow their bias to influence their interactions. They listen and avoid assumptions about the person that might influence how they receive the other person's suggestions, and they care more about finding a solution than whose idea the solution was.

When leaders lack compassionate communication, team performance can be adversely affected, most notably in three ways: energy, engagement, and exploration. Alex Pentland, award-winning data scientist and media arts and sciences professor, identifies these three key elements of communication in the *Harvard Business Review* article entitled "The New Science of Building Great Teams."[4]

Energy levels of a team are determined by the type of communication, such as face-to-face, video conference, phone, or email, and the frequency of that type of communication as well as how many people participate in the exchange. Very early in my career, I was put on a project without a sponsor and with an inexperienced project manager leading a multicultural team in the delivery of a content management system. Typically, a project should never be approved without an official sponsor, someone who takes ownership of the project and supports the project team. Without a formal sponsor for the project, the team lacked leadership beyond the project manager.

Project team meetings were often unorganized and disjointed, and as a result, agendas and meeting minutes were not always generated. When agendas were distributed by the team's project manager, the documents arrived within moments of the start of the meeting, thereby not providing the team enough time to review, comment, discuss, or prepare for the upcoming meetings. Members skipped meetings out of frustration, therefore information was not disseminated across the team in a timely manner, which precluded aligned decision-making, efficiencies, and overall progress. The team members' energy levels were very low.

Engagement levels are reflected by the distribution of energy throughout the team. On this project, the team spent zero time getting to know each other's customs and motivations, and team members rarely interacted outside of work. The project manager did not seem to possess the needed assertiveness or the desire to learn about the cultural traits of the team members. He kept to himself and rarely ventured out of his office. One or two team members often hijacked the meetings, leaving the remaining team members with not enough time to review and discuss their topics of importance. This fostered decreased engagement across the team. Team members became less likely to engage with one another outside team meetings to further explore and take deep dives into topics. Five months into the project, the team was three months behind schedule. Little had been accomplished in terms of initial planning, information gathering, and decision-making.

Exploration levels are measured by the energy between different teams. Because of the lack of leadership and the project team's low energy and low engagement, some members of the team sought out outside resources from other teams. This resulted in higher exploration levels, which served to reinforce the low engagement within the team.

Bottom line, the business not only incurred costs associated with resources, time, and materials, but also incurred costs in decreased team morale and development, subsequently affecting future projects and overall organizational effectiveness.

When leaders employ compassionate communication, they are able to ensure quality interaction among individuals on their teams, creating high levels of energy. High energy encourages engagement among team members, regardless of their differences, opening pathways for everyone involved to increase their cultural agility. This increased cultural agility will expand the way the team views the project and each other, and this may promote their curiosity to seek outside resources as another way to expand their perspective.

And it all begins with a relatable leader who recognizes the value of compassionate communication.

THE ETHICS OF LEADING

Ethics is about right and wrong, but from whose perspective? One component of compassionate communication that relatable leaders address is the ethics of leading diverse groups of people. I've been in many meetings where people disagreed on an approach to a project because of their differing work experiences. I've also been in one too many meetings where individuals fought over a solution because they firmly believed the other people were just plain wrong.

Many companies have a crisis of representation, with a dominant group of loud voices that do not accurately represent the sentiments of every voice in the organization. Accepting the dominant group's perspective without investigating whether it truly represents the whole can lead to stagnation or failure within that organization.

Relatable leaders understand the need to be fluid in how they communicate with their teams. They practice open communication and build trust with their employees through compassionate communication, and they focus on the three ways to be culturally responsive: culturally appropriate, culturally congruent, and culturally compatible.

By being culturally appropriate, relatable leaders are sensitive to all the cultures represented in the room and how those cultures influence an individual's interpretations of the interactions. By being culturally congruent, relatable leaders focus on the balance of cultures and how each culture might not align with others. To make the team culturally compatible, relatable leaders incorporate the strengths and differences of each culture to create a coexistence of cultures within the same space. But even with compassionate communication, misunderstandings can occur. Leaders need to approach a conflict not as a matter of right or wrong but as a matter of perspective.

According to ethics experts Manuel Velasquez, Claire Andre, and Thomas Shanks, SJ, and philosophy professor Michael J. Meyer, "Ethics refers to well-founded standards of right and wrong that prescribe what humans ought to do, usually in terms of rights, obligations, benefits to society, fairness, or specific virtue."[5] Ethical leadership provides a basic foundation for demonstrating how to be culturally responsive. In the Ethical Leadership course I teach to graduate students at Georgetown University, we explore the concept of moral integrity and the reasons some teams work and some are doomed to have ethical conflict from day one. I can't think of many people who would want to work with someone who is deemed ethically lacking, but the lesson we have to learn is that by practicing compassionate communication, we can enter each interaction with the understanding that different cultures have different ideas about what's right or how to behave. This also includes how we view ourselves and create an ethical framework on which we operate.

According to Susan Krauss Whitbourne, author of *The Search for Fulfillment*, we all need role models to motivate and inspire us. Children grow into adults who become role models for other children, and those adults who become supervisors, managers, or directors become role models for other adults. Anti-role models, those who engage in "acts of questionable ethics,"[6] reinforce negative behavior. We've probably all met at least one supervisor, manager, or director in our professional career who could be labeled an anti-role model. So how is ethicalness learned?

As Whitbourne suggests, ethics is formed in three ways:

1. What we learn as children is what guides how ethical we are as adults.
2. Employees learn vicariously from mentors in the workplace.
3. Employees observe executives' behavior as the standard of behavior needed to reach high-level positions.

Leaders often rely on situational awareness and societal norms to determine the best course of action. To do so, they focus on the positive values of their organizations and the society in which they live. By observing ongoing acceptable behaviors, what is right or wrong should become evident, but that's not always the case.

The phrase *back in the day* can be used to discuss moral principles that have changed over time because of someone else's perspective. For example, back in the day—the Spartan day—infanticide was not only accepted, but it was also expected. When boys turned seven years old, they were removed from their parents' homes. They were encouraged to steal food, and hazing and fighting was encouraged.[7]

From the Spartan's perspective, they were not living an unethical lifestyle. If you were a leader in Sparta, your moral principles would be grounded in producing the perfect soldier to protect your people.

Ethics and the discussion of ethical standards can elicit strong feelings. To understand your position on the ethics of leading, you must examine your personality type and leadership identity. Not everyone wants to lead a Fortune 100 company, but everyone should want to lead their own lives. Meaning, in understanding your personality type and leadership identity, you will be able to understand how best to interact with the people in the world around you.

Of course, there are a number of leadership behaviors that cast a dark shadow in the ethical space. Some of these include increasing employee workload while disregarding the interests of the key stakeholders, higher rates of absenteeism, humiliating and bullying employees, and claiming credit for the work of others. Craig E. Johnson, author of *Meeting the Ethical Challenges of Leadership*, calls these the behaviors of psychopaths and attributes them to faulty decision-making.

While it's disheartening to know that most people have encountered unethical behavior, these encounters are also learning experiences that help define who we are as individuals and as leaders. We will admit to thinking that sometimes an achievable ethical blueprint might not exist to correct the behavior; however, continual compassionate communication is key. When we enter each conversation with the intention of understanding where the other person is from or why they find their behavior acceptable, we have a better chance of understanding the situation.

Shopping Carts

Chief Stephanie Spell has been with the Collier County Sheriff's Office, a large public safety law enforcement agency, since 1987. She is the highest-ranking female chief and the second-in-command of a 1,300-member agency. When we mentioned Ethical Leadership to her, she shared with us the perfect example of her own ethical framework, and it starts with the shopping cart.

There are no rules or consequences to returning a shopping cart to a corral or store, at least not at this time. When you're in a parking lot, you can see people who shove their cart between cars without a care for the other person's vehicle or if the cart blocks an empty space. Returning a cart shows basic decency and doesn't take but a moment for most people. In Christine Hauser's *New York Times* article "Everyone Has a Theory About Shopping Carts," she mentions "carts as a test of character."[8] While Christine points out the various reasons people might not be able to return a cart, ultimately, the shopping cart theory shows a person's moral character.

When you're a leader, everybody looks to you. Not just in a crisis or an organizational way, but also in how you conduct yourself personally. As part of the command staff, Chief Spell takes that responsibility seriously. No matter what the weather, how late she's running, or how distracted she is, she returns the shopping cart to where it belongs.

Paul Levy

In 2002, Paul Levy took over the troubled Beth Israel Deaconess Medical Center. Sacha Pfeiffer, in an article for WBUR News, states, "For nearly a decade, Paul Levy was perhaps the best-known chief in Boston. He wrote a widely read blog and had had previous high-profile jobs in which he turned around troubled agencies."[9]

Many people who have studied this case (available through Harvard Business School's Case Collection) believe the level of communication that was created when Levy took the leadership role contributed to his success. Levy's moral profile at the time was integral to this accomplishment. The employees trusted him because of his transparency and incremental progress due to sacrifices made by the staff through his leadership. It was his interpretation of how to be transparent that created these pathways of communication. Additionally, the culture of the organization and Levy's ability to understand its importance played a vital role in his success.

In 2010, John Commins for HealthLeaders Media wrote, "Levy's Cautionary Tale: Don't Call For Transparency When Your Windows Are Dirty."[10] In the article, Cummins states that Levy was fined $50,000 for having "an improper personal relationship with a female subordinate." This shows how leaders should be held to a standard that makes all employees feel they are on the same footing, rather than being allowed to show favoritism.

Those around Levy thought his professional behavior reflected his moral profile. In fact, that belief might be the reason for the community's shock. The lifestyle of leaders and how their personal and professional behaviors align with each other, especially in the case of a man calling for transparency, is perhaps what made this resignation so startling. Maybe if he'd been more proactive in handling the fallout after his actions came to light, he might have been more readily forgiven for his lapse in judgment.

Certain qualities are ingrained in leaders, and those aspects of their personalities shouldn't be shut off at the end of the day. Additionally, Levy was committed to empowering others around him to continually learn and improve, and communication and transparency played vital roles in his success. The situation might have been different if the internet had not been a primary part of Levy's reason for being considered a great leader.

Still, Levy resigned. To some, his letter of resignation was somewhat ambiguous and did not adequately respond to the ongoing questions about his relationship, which he states in an interview with

Sacha Pfeiffer is "a private matter." Even if Levy would have addressed his lapse in judgment with the Beth Israel staff and asked for forgiveness, he might not have had the same authority or influence.

Too often people are only as respected as their moral code. A paperweight on my desk says: "When you're right, no one remembers. When you're wrong, no one forgets." Levy's downfall is an example of that saying. A hundred good deeds can be overshadowed by even the perception of unethical behavior.

Quite possibly Levy resigned because it wasn't worth it to him to continue to work in an environment where people mistrusted him or perceived him as immoral or unethical. He most likely recognized the almost impossible task of overcoming the dark mark on his reputation, and no matter how much more good he could do, he would spend too much time doing damage control than making positive gains.

Some students in my Ethical Leadership course at Georgetown University made great cases for why dating an employee does not cross an ethical line in corporate America. Others agreed that what made it shady was Levy's lack of transparency when his transparency in other areas was what made him a great leader in their eyes.

Overall, the behavior of a senior executive dating a junior employee and having the authority to promote them is considered a vague area within the human resources realm. Some companies have policies about the reporting structure and appropriateness of relationships, along with requiring documentation asking for the couple to be transparent. When you're in a leadership position, you can use the Levy case to caution the leaders around you about falling into this vague area of behavior.

It's critical for leaders to acknowledge how their actions could be perceived by others. An ethical leader, especially at the highest moments of their career, needs to recall how to effectively self-monitor. When you're in a situation where a CEO you know is portraying a loss of social intelligence or if you are the CEO in a related situation, you'll reflect back on this book and find solutions that will help you navigate the situation.

Leading ethically is not just about avoiding ethical transgressions. Leading ethically is also about how we—as leaders—ethically make decisions. Let's look at some situations where your decisions will reflect your moral code.

Trolleys

The trolley situation is a fictious example used to discuss ethical considerations in various trainings and courses. If you haven't heard of the trolley situation, here it is in brief: A trolley is speeding down the tracks in line to hit five oblivious workers. If you pull a lever, the trolley will then switch tracks, where it will hit one oblivious worker. Would you pull the lever?

Knowing nothing else except that a decision should be made, how would you act or not act? Acting would kill one worker but save five. Not acting would kill five workers.

In this situation, you're unaware of the identity of the individuals, professionally or personally. As leaders, you will face many situations where you may or may not have all the background information that you need to make what you feel is an informed decision. It's always interesting to note how people rationalize their actions.

In moral philosopher Judith Thomson's 1976 article titled "Killing, Letting Die, and the Trolley Problem," another scenario is introduced. Instead of pulling a lever to save the five workers, would you push a very large man into the path of the trolley to derail it and save the five workers?

The question of whether there is a difference between letting someone die and killing them matters. The more we discuss the ethical dilemma involved in these decisions, the more conflicted some of us may feel. Would it make a difference if any of the participants were children or women? For most of my graduate students, it would, and the main points of discussion revolve around the premise that killing is wrong. Their moral code is reflected through their positionality, and the idea that we should treat people the way we want to be treated. A deeper discussion examined the repercussions of acting against their moral code, and, more notably, who establishes the moral code. The ethics of leading challenges relatable leaders to use compassionate communication when establishing a code of conduct for those they influence.

LEADERSHIP IS A CHOICE

Becoming a relatable leader is a choice, and it comes with responsibilities. In intangible ways, we are all role models. In our daily lives, people will see how we behave, form opinions and judgments, and in some cases people will change for the better or the worse because of us. They may use our bad behavior to justify behaving badly themselves, or they may make note of our good behavior and try to mimic it.

Everyone leaves a trail of themselves made up of the mosaic of their life, pieces of experiences gathered since they were young, and people they looked up to as role models. So you as a leader and role model are a mosaic of all the role models you've encountered since birth. You will be challenged to make decisions, and those decisions will form the framework from which you will operate. Hopefully, as you're reading this book, you're understanding the central role your positionality and culture plays in becoming a relatable leader. Even if you don't supervise someone directly right now, you are still a leader in the way you behave, react, and perform in your current role.

Relatable leaders expand on their relatability and increase their awareness of the value of compassionate communication by approaching each interaction without judgment and with the intention of making a meaningful connection. They do this in the following ways:

* **Relatable leaders read about the cultural norms of different countries.** For example, a friend of ours who lived in Spain for many years shared with us that they eat pizza with a fork and knife. This pleased Marisa, because she prefers to eat pizza the same way, and this is one piece of information that makes her a little more relatable to many Spanish people we encounter.

* **Relatable leaders consider avoiding idioms or references to what could be considered common knowledge.** When they use them, they include a brief qualifier or explanation, so others may learn the phrase organically.

* **Relatable leaders listen to what others aren't saying.** They pay attention to nonverbal communication and micro signs to get a holistic sense of what the other person means to say.

* **Relatable leaders communicate openly, checking with the other person to make sure the message sent is the same one being received.**

* **Relatable leaders use their cultural agility to enter each interaction with compassion for where the other person is coming from.** This compassion provides a starting line for understanding why someone may act the way they act.

CHAPTER SIX REFLECTION

In this chapter's reflection, we'd like you to take a moment to think about the ways in which you communicate with others. In my professional experience, I've found the job of a project manager, and in fact most roles, is 90 percent communication, and ineffective communication has often destroyed morale on many teams. Relatable leaders use compassionate communication to add value to each exchange and create meaningful conversations.

The following questions will help you reflect on the interconnectedness of culture and communication:

- How do cultural norms and traditions impact communication and dialogue?
- What are the implications of globalization and culture on leadership?
- How does your communication style increase the energy levels on your team?
- How does your communication style increase engagement and foster exploration?

Now complete this phrase out loud or in the silence of your mind, and write it down:

By using compassionate communication, I will be able to better relate to . . .

7 The Leadership Lifestyle

The leadership lifestyle is a way of life where frames and lenses matter. How leaders frame themselves and others influences their behavior, and the lens leaders use to view situations impacts their actions. When leaders frame themselves as role models, mentors, and the ones setting examples, they accept the fact that they will have followers. Their followers will trust them to care for them. When leaders look through the lens of a leader, they see a give-and-take relationship. Leaders motivate and inspire, and they give back. They take risks, take charge, and take care.

The leadership lifestyle can mean different things to different people. There is no one model for the leadership lifestyle, and no one skill or set of skills to acquire. If we look at successful leaders, however, we see they live their lives in similar ways and share similar attitudes. They choose to be leaders, and they step into situations where leaders are needed.

In this chapter, we're going to focus on the leadership lifestyle by providing

* an examination of the leadership lifestyle through the lenses of role models and mentoring,
* ways to recognize you are the leader,
* a discussion of how leading by example works,
* ways to earn and gain trust,
* how caring for your followers leads to success, and
* a reflection upon ways your lifestyle aligns personally and professionally.

ROLE MODELS

My mom loved me when no one else wanted me. She was my first female role model, and she showed me how to be kind, how to be strong, and how to be fair. My whole approach to life changed the day I realized I was the role model. Way back when I first entered the classroom to teach middle schoolers language arts and literature, I taped a sign to the podium reminding me of the tremendous responsibility I decided to shoulder by becoming a teacher. The quote was by renowned psychologist Haim G. Ginott,[1] and it said:

> I've come to the frightening conclusion that I am the decisive element in the classroom. It's my personal approach that creates the climate. It's my daily mood that makes the weather. As a teacher, I possess a tremendous power to make a child's life miserable or joyous. I can be a tool of torture or an instrument of inspiration. I can humiliate or heal. In all situations, it is my response that decides whether a crisis will be escalated or de-escalated and a child humanized or dehumanized.

During my time in the classroom, I read that sign quite often, and when students used the podium for presentations, they would see it. When administrators or substitute teachers visited, they would read it and comment as well, and when I had the opportunity to speak to a group of new teachers, I pulled out the Ginott quote as part of my presentation, sharing with them that once the bell rang and the door to the classroom closed, it was just them and the children waiting to see what they'd do. Still, even then, even with the quotation taped to my podium, even with glowing evaluations and nominations for teaching awards, I didn't fully appreciate the fact that teaching is leading.

Teachers have a tremendous amount of influence over those who enter their classroom. I didn't think much about this until after I earned my doctorate and started working with graduate students, and about half a dozen people reached out to me and told me they wanted my life. They asked me how they could get to where I was, sought my advice for their own career path, and shared how my experiences influenced them. I influenced them—these men and women older and younger than me, white, and not outwardly marginalized. Me. An abandoned, adopted South Korean immigrant who never thought someone else would want to be me. And I fully realize that's not what they specifically meant, but the fact that people were saying they basically want to be me influenced me so deeply says a lot about me and my positionality.

This realization also showed me that I needed to reframe the way I viewed myself. When more than one person asked me why I wasn't taking advantage of my privilege, I replied that I never considered myself privileged. But if others wanted to know how I got to where I was, and how they could get there, too, then I needed to reposition myself as a role model and share with them the behaviors and actions I took on my path. I've since learned to appreciate how fortunate I am and how I can use what I've learned to help other people on their journey.

As I reflect on the years I've been blessed to live on this earth, and I make connections with others who share similar goals, I have come to this conclusion: No matter how you label me—Marisa Cleveland, EdD, or Dr. Marisa Cleveland—no matter which title you use—wife, daughter, sister, niece, author, literary agent, executive director, professor, or trustee—I don't have a job; I have a purpose.

REPRESENTATION

KL Burd became a writer because he understood the value of representation. As a young child he loved reading but never saw any kids that looked like him in his favorite books. Once he had kids of his own, he discovered that he could do for them what no one had done for him.

As a writer he understood that he was the CEO of his own career, and he worked hard to study his craft and make connections in the industry. In addition to sharing his poetry and creative writing on his website and speaking on leadership, KL aimed to create a brand that gave him the most reach in regard to getting his words out to the world. After 130 unsuccessful attempts, he was able to connect with literary agents who valued and understood his work and aspirations.

During KL's first stab at pitching his manuscript to agents who might agree to represent him and help him find a publisher, he queried twenty-five agents and received no full requests. Determined to plow forward, because failure was not an option, KL decided he would query a minimum of one hundred agents before reassessing his writing journey. This time, however, he received twenty-four requests for his full manuscript. This simple act of people asking him to show them more pushed him forward.

As the son of immigrants from the Caribbean, he had the privilege of growing up in various states and overseas. His dad was in the US Army during KL's childhood, and that took him from New Jersey to Kansas to Germany to Hawaii. During that time, he had many role models around him, as the military framed his entire life in the view of leadership. He was taught that he was not only going to be a leader, but also that he was a leader in that moment. Role models gave him something to strive for.

From those days on army bases to his adult days, many of his role models were his coaches. Sports taught him so much about leadership, and after his playing days were over, he became a coach and educator. It was throughout this time as an educator that he developed his thoughts on leadership.

KL figured out he was a leader after he left college and found himself in many situations in which he could lead. People told him that he was a natural-born leader, and he took that on.

At some point, he became confident in his leadership skills, and after many years, two things helped him figure out what a good leader is: reading and real-life examples. A friend had told him that he would be the same person ten years from now except for the books he read and the people he met. He wasn't reading any leadership books at the time, so he started digging in. He was a coach and wanted to know how to better lead his team.

Sadly, KL passed unexpectedly in November of 2021, but during his time on Earth, he served on executive boards, chaired the Violence Prevention and Second Chances subcommittee on the executive council for President Obama's My Brother's Keeper initiative in the Greater Austin Area, and volunteered at various local churches.

For KL, role models were an aiming point to guide him in the direction of his dreams, even if some of his role models were viewed from afar. He thought the best thing that can happen to a leader was when their role model became their mentor. When you have a role model willing to walk through the steps with you, share their resources, and challenge you to be better, that is where real change happens.

More than just having a story to tell, he wanted to make space at the table for those coming up behind him. He envisioned a market where books by authors of color fill the bookshelves of every bookstore and the homes of children. Because of this he created a community for Black speculative fiction writers and participated in various mentoring programs. He didn't just want a spot at the big table, he also wanted the space to create his own table—one that would celebrate the diversity he had wished to see as a kid. KL was a prime example of a role model living the leadership lifestyle.

MENTORING

One aspect of living the leadership lifestyle is to consider the way knowledge sharing occurs in both your personal life and professional life. Very rarely will someone care more about your goals than you do. But as a leader you want to find a way to get others to care enough about you and your goals to help you build your dreams. Hopefully, those supporting you will find ways to achieve their goals along the way. As motivational speaker Tony Gaskins Jr.'s subtitle to his book *The Dream Chaser* states, "If you don't build your dream, someone will hire you to help build theirs."[2]

As a leader, people will look *to* you and *at* you. Having mentors—or a lack of them—can make a huge difference in how you dream. Positive mentors influence attitudes and behaviors. Just as leadership involves influencing others, so, too, do mentors. Mentoring is the next step after realizing you're a role model.

When I first thought I wanted to write a book, I had no idea what the process was. Way back when, the queries were still paper letters mailed to a literary agent's office, and I didn't even know about national writers' groups and their local chapters. So it's really thanks to fellow writer Judi McCoy and her attitude toward me that helped shape my attitude now.

I met her at a gymnastics event where we were both judges. When I saw her reading a student paper in the lounge, I asked if she was a teacher like me, and when she said she was a romance writer, I blurted out that I've always wanted to write a book. She smiled and asked how she could help me, and she shared what she knew. She became a trusted adviser, and because of Judi, I found a supportive community and the potential of actually writing a book. I had started so many projects but never completed a full manuscript until after I met her.

Judi's attitude of helping others seeped into other areas of my life, and as I immersed myself in the publishing industry, I transitioned from teaching students to working at a literary agency. One of my initiatives involved implementing our internship program.

Nicole Resciniti, the agency's president, has been an incredible mentor for her team and for the interns from day one. At the end of one of the internship terms, Nicole promoted one intern, Elisa Houot, to junior agent. I'd had such a wonderful time working with Elisa over the past term, and we immediately planned ways for her to build her career.

Elisa's dream and goal since she started working in publishing was to be able to start building her list of authors, and she was ready. When reflecting upon the start of her agenting career, Elisa noted, "The months of training I had before that moment helped me be prepared in a professional perspective—I knew what to look for in a manuscript, what to ask an author before offering representation, how to send a book out on submission, Marisa's intern training had covered everything."[3] One thing Elisa hadn't expected was the nervousness that came with all of this. The sudden responsibility of taking on an author, being the one advocating for them in a difficult and constantly moving industry, was not one she took lightly.

As a new agent, she needed approval to sign new clients. After my literary assistant read a fantastic query from a writer and alerted me, I sent it to Elisa for her review. We met with the author together, and that author became Elisa's first client. Over the next few months, I invited Elisa to editor meetings, read manuscripts for her potential clients, and worked with her to create opportunities for success. Fast forward several months, and that first client Elisa signed is Elisa's first sale to an editor at a major publishing house. Now Elisa is not only a literary agent with a solid client list, but she is also the agency's French subrights agent.

Her success feels like my success, and I'm so proud to have been a part of her journey. I learned so much about being a mentor by living a leadership lifestyle through supporting her in her work. I was happy to learn the effect this had on Elisa. She said, "Being able to have Marisa in my corner, coming with me to my first author calls and even taking the lead the first few times, helped me feel much less nervous and hesitant."[4]

Nicole's constant words of encouragement and her faith in what Elisa could accomplish did, without a doubt, play a part in Elisa's successes. Good mentorship prepared her for the job, wins, and accomplishments, but also and most importantly, it prepared her for the losses and the disappointments. As with any industry, things don't always go as planned in publishing: contracts fall through, authors choose other agents, a project we truly believed in doesn't sell . . . but Elisa was able to benefit from Nicole's experiences, the internship, and the mentorship.

Altony Lee III, director of university relations for Florida Gulf Coast University, believes "executive leaders must be willing to mentor mid-level managers to expose them to new opportunities and realities."[5] He notes that there are many programs that offer networking as its most significant benefit. Those are great for natural extroverts, but for introverts, it can be a disappointment. He was shy and introverted, so his growth stemmed from his mentors pushing him to speak up and share his opinion. Now Altony is involved with his community by mentoring students at Florida State University; participating in Leadership Collier, Leadership Florida, and doing speaking engagements for student clubs and organizations, chambers, Rotary Clubs, and other community groups; serving as an active member of the Florida Chamber of Commerce; and sitting on half a dozen boards.

When relatable leaders cultivate other relatable leaders, stronger teams emerge, and there is a positive impact on employee satisfaction and performance. Mentors share their knowledge and experiences, and they empower those around them to embark on their own journey while still receiving guidance and support. When mentees learn how to think critically, immerse themselves in their lives, wake up, and create and take risks, then progress is made.

DOES LEADING BY EXAMPLE REALLY WORK?

Yes. Yes, it does.

On Wednesday, March 17, 2021, I opened Twitter to a single tweet from Alessandra Balzer: "Matched. Will someone match me for $50?" It was in reply to a tweet from Alexandra Levick that read "I donated $50 to Heart of Dinner in NYC, a nonprofit that has been particularly important in helping to feed older Asian American folks throughout the pandemic. Who will match me?"

It didn't take long to discover the cause of this call to action. Twitter news provided several links to reliable sources, and the short of it was another violent crime against Asians in America. The fear I have lived with in the back of my brain came to the forefront, and my visceral reaction stalled all forward momentum. Every terror I had ever imagined was happening to those who look like me. On a daily basis. All over the United States. Meaning, there was not one place I could go where I would feel safe and secure. Had there ever been? I'd experienced microaggressions and outright racism in pretty much every place I've ever lived.

So when Kidlit Against Anti-AAPI Racism held an online auction fundraiser, I donated a one-month mentorship that included manuscript critiques, Zoom sessions, and a Q and A on anything related to . . . anything for an author without an agent. I donated my time because I consider it my most valuable asset, especially given everything that was going on in the world right then.

The violence against Asians was being spotlighted in the media, but I volunteered my time, put myself out there, despite my fears. If I really believed in the leadership lifestyle, I couldn't hide or ignore the chance to support an organization dedicated to helping educate the public and supporting marginalized communities. This auction not only raised money and awareness, but it also provided an expanded inclusive space for everyone to contribute to the cause. After I tweeted that I had donated this item for the auction, others messaged me saying they would also donate or bid on items, and that showed me that I'd inspired others to step up and help, even if they weren't directly a part of the Asian American Pacific Islander community. Most importantly, I was able to work with a wonderful writer for a month and help him on his path to publication.

So let me return to the purpose of this section: leading by example works.

Why is this so important for emerging leaders to understand? Because on that terrifying day back in March of 2021, Alessandra Balzer tweeted, I saw her message, then I followed her example, and then someone else followed mine. I also checked in with a group on social media for adopted Koreans, like me, and one topic of discussion was how many of our white families checked in to see if we were okay. The answer: none. Same with our white friends and colleagues. They acted as though it were any other normal day for them. And for them, it was. They didn't understand how the violence inflicted against Asians impacted how we perceive the world we live in. That's not an accusation. It's a fact. But we, as leaders of our lives, shared with our white families and friends our concerns and fears, and then some understood.

Because one leader sent one tweet, others followed that lead, and then they themselves became leaders in raising awareness.

This is the power of leading by example.

As the chief operating officer for Gulf Coast International Properties, Vicki Tracy has worked with both role models and anti-role models. She believes a good leader walks their talk and inspires others to be the best versions of themselves. One of her former bosses modeled servant leadership so effectively that she now embodies the servant leadership lifestyle. Tracy chairs multiple community events and sits on the board of various nonprofits. She doesn't behave one way at work and another way at home. She walks her talk, and she never gives someone something to do that she isn't willing to do herself. She's an inspiration to the up-and-coming leaders in the community, and, most importantly, she understands the critical need for succession planning.

Established leaders need to identify emerging leaders and create pathways to help them cultivate their talents today so they can lead five or ten years down the road. She's witnessed corporations enter crisis mode when they didn't have anyone in their current organization who could step in to lead them through that difficulty. One simple question helps her identify emerging leaders: Do you want to be in the play, direct the play, or be in the audience?

If someone desires to play a particular role, she can teach them what they need to know to take on the responsibilities of that role. She recently hired a professional baseball player who didn't like his career path and wanted to learn about real estate. He was born and raised in Southwest Florida, and he had every leadership quality she considers crucial for his success. So how does he get to the next level? He needs some product knowledge and time. It takes time to develop leaders, and it takes mentors willing to spend that time.

If someone isn't called to be a leader but is taught leadership skills, they probably can't be taught the most crucial component of being a successful leader: caring. Think back to the prerequisites for becoming a leader and to your final reflection in chapter one. You want to be a leader because you care about something. Whatever that something is, it propels you forward in your journey.

During lunch on a sunny afternoon, Tracy referenced a *Wall Street Journal* survey in which researchers discovered that people left jobs because they didn't feel valued, wanted, or needed. Oftentimes, it wasn't about the money or the need to be right. They just wanted to be heard. So if bad bosses are those who don't make employees feel valued, wanted, or needed, then it seems like it would be an easy solution to become a good boss. All you have to do is make your employees feel valued, wanted, or needed.

All you have to do is care.

Years ago, before he was the president of Hodges University, John Meyer was working at a car dealership, and his service manager was a horrible individual. Even though he was a service manager, he knew nothing about repairing automobiles, which might have been okay if he knew how to care about his team. He didn't.

As Meyer recalls, the automobile technician expected the service manager to respect them as a person and for their skills and knowledge about how to examine, diagnose, and repair an automobile. At the very least, they hoped the service manager would not insult them by pretending they were subhuman.

This particular service manager didn't care that the technicians were paid in six-minute increments, used their own tools in each bay, and had very real skin in the game—meaning, if they proposed the wrong diagnosis, they would have to do some of the work they missed for free. Instead of caring about his team and trusting their skill sets, he would say in front of the customer that the diagnosis was wrong, and he would figure out what the real problem was, even when the technician was right.

Without the feeling of being cared for or cared about, technicians left. They counted on their service managers to sell the work to the customers rather than undermine the diagnostic work they had done.

Meyer stayed less than a year with that bad boss, but he didn't leave without learning two valuable lessons: his own worth and what motivated him and what discouraged him. He was in a position to learn from what was happening to him, so he wouldn't turn out like that bad boss, and because of that experience, he sees even bad examples as good examples if they teach what not to do to someone else.

Fortunately, he did have a great boss to set a better example for him as he continued to form his own leadership style. This guy— Bruno—was a manager at the grocery store Publix before moving to New Jersey to work as a car salesman. According to Meyer, Bruno was "such a cool guy." When the dealership offered Bruno the chance to run the service department, he admitted he didn't know anything about the automobile service industry. He did know how to care for his employees, however.

Bruno took the time to talk to everyone and learn about each person's relative ability, intelligence, skill set, and work ethic. He considered which person's particular people skills or personalities would align best with certain customers. This strategy was fabulously successful, and the dealership almost never sold something the customer didn't need.

Meyer attributes Bruno's success to being honest about not knowing about the technical aspects of automobile repair and relying on the employees to be honest and educate him. He cared enough to get to know his team and could defend them in their area of expertise, if necessary, because he could trust that they knew what they were doing.

EARNING AND GAINING TRUST

How do you get to the point of trusting your people enough to defend them to anyone—the general public, the general manager, the owner of the store, or other management?

Trusting others comes from wanting to get to know them and caring about them. If you just want to show up, manage some people, and go home, then leadership may not be right for you. You have to want to talk—and listen—to your team.

In an interview for this book, Meyer said, "Probably the hardest part about management—and by extension leadership—is talking to people. It's getting to know them. More than that, it's being able to relate to them."[6] He further shared that he believes it's a real skill set if someone can talk to an attorney at 10:00 AM and a janitor at 11:30 AM and make them both feel comfortable in that person's company. In order to connect with other people, you have to talk to them and use language and experiences they can understand and relate to.

Why do you work here? What do you get out of your job? What parts do you like or not like? What about your coworkers? What about your work space? These are the types of questions a leader should ask their employees. It almost doesn't matter what the leader asks as long as they're asking about their employees. Engaging over these types of questions gives insight into who the employees are and what attitude they hold, and this builds understanding. With a foundation of understanding, a leader can defend employees in the areas of their expertise because he's cared enough to get to know them.

Beyond earning and gaining trust among leaders and their teams, relatable leaders must know how to identify emerging leaders. The best part of Meyer's job is developing emerging leaders. He developed his leadership competencies by observing. He observed the people he worked for and learned what was effective and what was ineffective about their leadership styles. As an adult, he returned to college and observed the professors and learned how they handled the content as well as managed the classroom. As an administrator for a vocational school, he observed the director and admired how she would listen to everyone.

Now as a leader himself, observing is the method he uses to identify emerging leaders. The first thing he looks for is a sense of humor. He believes humor is an expression of native intelligence. If you're going to lead people, you must be intelligent.

In addition to these getting-to-know-you queries, Meyer watches people over time. He watches how they comport themselves in various situations and circumstances. He observes if they know what to say and how to say it. If they are sincere or humorous. If they can diffuse a potentially toxic or explosive situation. If they can deliver bad news or cheer someone up. He identifies people who excel in these areas and encourages them. He shows them how they can take on more responsibility and what life would be like in a leadership role.

Chief Stephanie Spell identifies emerging leaders by their work ethic and dependability. What started as a need to work nights, beginning as the midnight shift 911 dispatcher, while her daughter was young morphed into Spell finding her passion. As a young adult, she never sought out leadership roles, but as the oldest of three and the only girl, she often ended up in a pseudo leadership role. With a strong work ethic imparted on her from her parents and grandparents, and blessed with a good dose of common sense, she was able to progress through the agency in leadership roles in communications.

When discussing whether leaders are made or born, she thinks it's a lot of both. People look to you for guidance when you have a strong work ethic and are dependable. Over the years, she's developed an eye for spotting emerging leaders, and they all share one trait in common: Emerging leaders are fearless. They are especially not afraid

* to step up and participate. Whether it's an event or an incident or a crisis, emerging leaders are available and initiate participation.
* of responsibility. They take responsibility when they're wrong, and they take initiative when something needs to be handled, whether professionally or personally.
* to work hard and be accountable. If they say they're going to do something, they do it. Being dependable means others can count on you and trust you to be there when you say you're going to be there.

Even though Spell operates within the confines of a paramilitary organization with a clear chain of command, she's still witnessed plenty of de facto leaders. They are selected by their peers, and they've taken responsibility for their actions. That accountability and responsibility is a huge factor for her, since that creates trust. De facto leaders have built trust with their peers, and when she spots an emerging leader she can trust, she supports them in their leadership journey and encourages them to do the things needed to be done to be recognized as a leader.

So how does she spot these emerging leaders? By their level of commitment. Commitment shows the level of investment they are making in their career. Are they part of the organizational culture? Are they interested, trustworthy, and responsible? Have they stepped up to the plate in any program or crisis? If they have, she supports them as best she can, making sure they are exposed to training and development opportunities. If she sees an article or reads a book that is relevant, she shares that with them. She shares the qualities she's observed in them that will make them a good leader, and she does a lot of confidence building. Since the agency has such a regimented selection process for hiring and promoting, and no one did any confidence building for her, she's found her support to be a positive way to encourage emerging leaders as they establish themselves.

Without the external confidence building when she was moving up through the ranks, she had to prove she was an exceptional leader to herself as well as to others. By remaining authentic to herself and not compromising what she believed in, she persevered, even though many times it was difficult and she almost got fired. Still, she had a deep sense of commitment. When the time arrived for her to step into the first civilian chief position, she already knew how it could be done.

With the combination of core values and innate skills, she was able to realize her goal of being chief. She's had countless hours of leadership training and learned specific things from each opportunity, but leadership doesn't start in a vacuum. For Spell, it started with family and values, and her own goals and authenticity. The continuum of success is giving back by turning around and giving a hand to those coming up.

CARING FOR YOUR FOLLOWERS

Because leadership has a close relationship with influence, one of the responsibilities of having followers is to take care of them. Marilyn Santiago, partner and CMO of Creative Architectural Resin Products and president of Sunshine Integrated Solutions, is a dynamic, driven, and creative marketing and communications professional. She's a multifaceted and accomplished executive with a well-established reputation as a trustworthy leader in the US Hispanic and Southwest Florida markets. At an early age, she activated a group of about ten friends from her neighborhood to pick a fight with their neighbors so they would stop being mean to them. She declared war and got everybody excited. Then she assigned kids to stop traffic so they could cross a major intersection. As they were about to cross, her mother and a few other parents showed up and gave them a major whipping, frustrating their plans for war.

Despite the negative connotation of her actions, that day, four-year-old Santiago became a leader. She shared her intentions with the group, inspired them, assigned responsibilities, and led them to be grounded for about a week. Sometimes actions have consequences, but she learned a valuable lesson that framed her later years: everyone has the potential to be leaders, but some just don't know they have it.

Those who want to lead successfully are authentic, passionate, and inspiring. After graduating from college, she was the operations manager for four radio stations in Puerto Rico. Her first day at work was February 1, and by June she had produced her very first major music festival. Her event budget equaled $0, so she had to make everything happen by trading advertising (radio spots) for products and services such as stage, sound, transportation, vendor booths, security, talent, catering, water, and liquor. She even threw in a fireworks show and had the hottest artist of that time parachute into the festival!

It was not easy, but her team made it happen. The team members wore many different hats. They got dirty setting up the stage, putting together the booths, cleaning . . . they did everything. Everybody did what they were assigned to do, and when others needed help, they all helped each other because they cared. And because they cared, the event was a major success.

CHAPTER SEVEN REFLECTION

In this chapter's reflection, we'd like to revisit a story the spiritual guru Ram Dass told in his 1988 lecture on spiritual work in the United States, "Promises and Pitfalls of the Spiritual Path"[7]:

When a person thus loses herself or himself, she or he immediately finds themself in the service of all that lives. It becomes their delight and recreation . . . It reminds me of the story of the pig and chicken that are walking down the street, and they're hungry and they want breakfast, and they come to a restaurant, and they start to go in. And the pig says, "I'm not going in there." "Why not?" "Because there's a sign that says Ham and Eggs." The chicken says, "Oh, come on. We'll have something else." Pig says, "Look, it's fine for you. All they want is a contribution from you. From me they want total surrender. They want everything."

This story has been used for countless commitment situations, including marriage and other intense endeavors. Leadership is a choice, and caring is a prerequisite for becoming a leader. It's also a total surrender to a leadership lifestyle. It's not acting one way at home and another with friends and another at work. It's also not something that happens overnight.

In this chapter's reflection, we'd like you to consider ways you can make small changes until your leadership style matches your lifestyle, and you have totally surrendered to the leadership lifestyle.

Reflect on the following:

- Who do you consider to be your role models and why?
- Who are you mentoring or who could you be mentoring right now?
- Who are your followers? Do you know why they follow you? How do you build them up?
- What does *leading by example* mean to you?
- In what ways and in which situations do you act differently when you're at home, out with friends, and at work?

Now complete this phrase out loud or in the silence of your mind, and write it down:

I will embrace the leadership lifestyle in the following ways . . .

8 Nonhierarchical Leadership

Some years ago, I managed a project to deliver new functionality to a land management system that senior management had imposed along with an aggressive deadline. The complexity of the new functionality required my team to work long hours and during major holidays. To meet the deadline, the software update would potentially reduce the quality of the final product. Furthermore, acquiring vendor resources represented a major bottleneck, threatening our ability to complete the project on time. The work involved extensive negotiations, purchase orders, and concessions to meet the deadline.

As someone who places value on my team's well-being, I never use whether someone is the first one in and the last one out as a characteristic to assess someone's skill set or worth. Understanding the commitment that would be needed for us to meet the promises made by senior management, I asked many questions of our senior sponsor to determine the business need and what drove the aggressive deadline.

One of my key values is the need to associate my work with a purpose for the greater good, so I wanted to rationalize the need for the aggressive deadline for myself and for my team. Senior management's responses revealed that personal edification and politics played the main role in the decision for this system enhancement. The senior manager had promised (in fact, bragged) to several key external stakeholders (owners of multimillion dollar companies) that the organization could deliver this new functionality within a short time frame. This knowledge disappointed me but didn't deter me from my job.

In the end, we delivered the system on time. But what I won't forget is the spirit of cohesion, collaboration, and comradery our team members developed on our path to success. There were plenty of long nights, overtime work, and unhappy family members, but the experience strengthened us as a team. I understood the personal sacrifices my team members chose to make by working beyond what was expected. Even though I disliked the reasons behind the change, I never expressed my distaste for it in front of my team. Instead, we all committed to the long-term goal—we were helping our constituencies with functionality that could save them time and money. We were working to improve the quality of documents submitted to our agency.

By exercising the qualities of being self-aware, mission driven, and focused on the long-term results, I believed our department could transform from good to great. By learning to remain calm and inspire, especially in times of change (for example, workforce reductions), I hoped my team felt valued.

Relatable leaders practice compassionate communication with their employees in order to build trust. Our senior management could have brought value to the team by associating work with a purpose for the greater good, forging a spirit of cohesion, collaboration, and comradery in order to build the team to reach success.

Since relatable leaders view leadership as nonhierarchical, I found that my team had many leaders willing to step up and take ownership of the project so we would all succeed. Relatable leaders understand that leaders are found at all levels of the organization, and this is reflected in the way relatable leaders view and treat others. They recognize that even if a person is not considered an official leader holding an official title in a specific job, that person is still a leader in other ways. This attitude manifests in the ways relatable leaders engage with their family, friends, community, and workplace, and in this case, it illustrates that even if we didn't have relatable leaders at the helm, we could choose to step up to meet a difficult deadline.

Change doesn't happen if you stay in your lane. In this chapter, we're going to focus on nonhierarchical leadership by providing

* an exploration of the concept that leadership is nonhierarchical,
* a look at how relatable leadership manifests with the community and in organizations,
* a discussion of community leadership development programs,
* explaining the value of sustainability, and
* exploring ways to identify and promote nonhierarchical leadership.

LEADERS AT ALL LEVELS

Leaders are embedded within our lives at all levels. Relatable leaders see past titles, so they don't limit someone else's range of growth. Our titles—*mom, dad, analyst, manager, director, president, COO*—might help us clarify our job duties, but they don't determine whether we are leaders. Everyone can be a leader, and leaders are found at all levels of an organization, regardless of their position on the organizational chart. Relatable leaders understand this concept, which benefits them, their organization, and their community in two ways:

1. They don't get stuck in their roles, which means they don't allow others to get stuck in theirs either.
2. They understand that learning is a continual process, just as becoming an effective leader is a continual process. At all levels of leadership, leaders are continually learning and looking for new ways to make themselves and those around them better.

Early in my career with Accenture, I had the opportunity to work with an amazing leader who embraced nonhierarchical leadership. After I finished graduate school, Accenture hired me as a consultant, and, hierarchically, our teams consisted of analysts, consultants, managers, and partners. While we each had our specific job function, my manager on this project, Jay Jaiprakash, expected me to take ownership of my piece of the project, and from the start, he treated me like a leader. This was more than autonomy. This was my manager realizing that leaders are found at every level of an organization. It didn't matter that I was a consultant and he was a manager because he also displayed a cultural agility that inspired me. The way he communicated to each person on our team was individualized for that person.

As one of the youngest and newest consultants, and given my positionality of being born and raised in another country, I wasn't immediately familiar with some of the sports references used during the meetings, like "hit it out of the ballpark" and "level the playing field." Jay took the time to make eye contact with me seeking confirmation on whether I needed clarification when we were in meetings, and this showed me my ability to participate in the conversation mattered to him. Another guy on our team laughed when he didn't know the answer to something, and I noticed how Jay took that verbal cue as a way to ask more discovery questions from the client until we could all form an answer. The balance with which Jay used his cultural agility to treat us as valuable contributors on the team gave us a sense of ownership of the project. Reflecting back on this experience, I can appreciate the time he took getting to know each of our communication styles so he could extrapolate the best results from us.

Jay could have ignored our cues when something wasn't immediately clear to us and taken over the meetings, turning them into a one-man show, but he chose to find ways for us to feel as though we were not only a part of the team, but also individuals whose opinions and knowledge mattered. Jay understood that *leaders* and *followers* are not static terms. Instead, leaders and followers are fluid in their positions. In this case, our manager knew when to elaborate on what "the home stretch" meant so I could provide accurate details to the client. This not only showed Jay's ability to relate to what I might be feeling, but it also showed how he viewed leadership as nonhierarchical. The project was a success because of the collaborative efforts of the entire team of leaders.

In General Stanley McChrystal's book *Team of Teams*, he introduces the reader to a collective consciousness that aligns with his idea that leadership is best when it's collaborative. Collective consciousness uses shared learning in real time—for example, holding open-ended conversations among the senior leadership team during an update, and allowing all members of the organization to see problems being solved so they can learn from the decisions being made and build on their decision-making skills. In the book, he mentions shared consciousness and the need for transparency to reduce the silos that prevent an unobstructed view. This environment of transparency allows for everyone to see what is happening and where they fit in the complex system. While there are still different levels of leadership, they all share the same space. This is just one piece of changing the way people have viewed and practiced leadership—from a solo endeavor to a collective one.

From my early experience with Jay and while on other projects with Accenture, I learned that being a leader requires facing the expectation that you become better, do more, and create. Leading entails forward momentum, innovation, and looking at things differently than others have before you.

During one event where I spoke with business students at the University of Maryland, I made the statement that you don't need to wait until you reach your leadership potential to consider pathways to help others. Because leaders are found at all levels of an organization, no matter where you are on your path to becoming a leader, you're already part of many larger systems, and one of those systems is your community.

Nonhierarchical leadership manifests throughout your community. There's the customer service representative who is also the youth cheerleading coach, the car salesman who volunteers as the team lead for the local food pantry, the information technology specialist who chairs a walkathon, and the business analyst who is a volunteer service leader for the Girl Scouts. Relatable leaders see how leaders are found throughout a community and also become community leaders.

Joe Raelin, management and organizational development expert, states, "No one knows the practice better than the practitioner who must in relation to others negotiate and arrange the objects of his or her own practice."[1] Nourishing your community is that practice. You are the trustee of your community. Community development is focused on the process of improving the lives of the community residents. There is a positive impact on communities when community development focuses on relationship building and collaboration among community leaders. Therefore, it is essential for communities to develop leaders into active participants in community development, and those leaders must be trained to address challenges and promote local strengths.

This is the reality of leadership. Relatable leaders support the creation of sustainable, positive change. They see how their lives extended beyond the silo of just themselves. They consider others around them and acknowledge that they operate in complex systems. While working at Accenture, our leaders made a conscious effort to share with us ways to volunteer within the community. But beyond asking us to volunteer our time by pouring wine at a charity event or painting renovated homes for those who experienced homelessness, our leaders also challenged us to bring others to join us. I learned valuable lessons in leadership and influence through these experiences. And while it widened the network of people I normally interact with, more importantly I gained a sense of responsibility to my community.

LEADERSHIP DEVELOPMENT WITHIN COMMUNITIES

Communities can be classified by proximity (your neighbors), by geography (your town or city), virtually (social media groups with shared interests), by values (your religion), and by many other factors. As you think about your leadership development, consider your geographical community. Who are the people you live near, shop next to, and support with your tax dollars? Where do you go for recreation within a close radius to your home? How far do you drive to get to work if you work outside your home? Who are the people working in the service industries? This is your community.

During Marisa's doctoral studies, she read numerous articles about communities and the challenges they face. Among those challenges, some communities struggle with

* crime,
* limited access to high-quality education,
* health care services,

* a lack of resources to meet the growing demands of the community,
* an aging population with fewer wealthy residents,
* difficult living conditions, and
* cultural differences that further impede community development.

Of even more concern are the most pressing obstacles prohibiting positive community development: the lack of leaders with the skills and knowledge to lead a community and tackle issues that will improve their community's quality of life. Community leaders may not know how to conduct a meeting, discuss uncomfortable community issues with civil discourse, or even involve stakeholders in the decision-making process. Some community leaders may not understand how they operate within a complex system.

Leadership development programs enhance the motivation, soft skills, and skills transfer of organizational leaders. Such programs are collaborative, layered, and behavior enhancing. While we believe effective leaders are found not just at the top but throughout an organization, individual leaders rarely implement complex changes on their own. As a result, by embracing a collaborative leadership approach, leaders are better able to handle formidable challenges. This argument sets the premise for investigating how leadership development moves beyond the individual competencies toward a holistic view of developing leaders.

Community leadership emphasizes the empowerment of the citizens to contribute their input and opinions while negating the traditional top-down problem-solving approach. Beyond elected and local officials, who are the leaders empowered to make decisions for the community? Does your community have a Kiwanis club, a Rotary Club, a Lions Club, any civic associations, homeowner associations, or other organizations? These are your community leaders. These individuals are working toward a common goal—to develop a positive, sustainable community. The concept of community leadership includes developing local solutions to reflect the current and future needs of the citizens. Unlike traditional leaders in organizations, community leaders tend to share a sense of service and change agent roles, and this role often stems from an identification of an issue within the community.

In 2015, educational administration experts Jia G. Liang and Lorilee R. Sandmann conducted a study to explore leadership in the context of fostering community engagement using the data from 224 Carnegie-classified community-engaged institutions. The findings indicated that community engagement is not limited to one institution or organization, or even to a specific department. Community engagement occurs among other campuses and communities, where multiple organizations or groups focus on coming together to achieve a common goal. Thus, community development requires community leadership that extends across all industries in the community, including education, the private sector, nonprofits, and government.

Many leaders take charge of their lives and the bigger picture through participation in a community leadership development program.

COMMUNITY LEADERSHIP DEVELOPMENT PROGRAMS

Does your community have a leadership development program? We interviewed several community leaders about community leadership and leadership development programs and share their insights throughout this chapter.

When City of Everglades City Councilman Michael McComas sat on the Greater Naples Chamber of Commerce's board of directors, he went to a retreat and learned about community leadership development programs.

These programs are designed for leaders who want to make an impact on their community and in their professional lives, and they encourage leaders across all industries to participate and collaborate in creating solutions for the betterment of the community.

After seeing the benefits of having a community leadership development program in the community, McComas cofounded Leadership Collier for the Collier County and Southwest Florida regions. According to McComas, Leadership Collier emerged through the Greater Naples Chamber of Commerce to bring together a network of diverse industry leaders who would help bridge the gaps in the community and provide local leaders with the knowledge and opportunity to create sustainable community development. He saw a need within his community, and he acted to implement a solution.

Community leadership development programs not only enhance an individual's leadership skills, but also cultivate communication skills, knowledge, and relationships. In this way, residents contribute to the solutions for their communities and learn the leadership competencies necessary for sustainable progress they might not otherwise encounter. The empowerment of community residents contributes to community success, and the purpose of community leadership education is to make participants active in community leadership opportunities.

In general, these programs are most often sponsored by chambers of commerce, private nonprofit agencies, local governments, and higher education institutions, all designed to inspire citizens to engage in civic leadership. While each community leadership development program is uniquely designed for the local community, the program curriculum generally includes instruction through experiential learning, community tours, and networking opportunities. Participants learn about their community's history, resources, and challenges, as well as explore the various industries, such as arts and culture, education, government, health care, and law enforcement, which places the participants in direct contact with the community and facilitates the learning process.

Community leadership development programs that are aligned with the local community's challenges connect leaders among industries when the programs are designed to enhance the leadership competencies of the participants, help leaders convert followers into leaders, and train individuals lacking a leadership title to become leaders. Through community leadership development programs, participants build relationships with other participants and professionals affiliated with the programs, enabling them to participate in networks beyond their family and friends.

Amanda Beights, senior director of leadership programs for the Leadership Collier Foundation, said, "When one continuously works to serve others in need, in whatever capacity that may be, I believe that is when one truly becomes a leader. Working beyond what serves you best, both personally and professional, is the pinnacle of leadership in my opinion."[2]

Because of their unique positioning within a community, community leadership development programs play a pivotal role in improving communities, such as

* building a peaceful society,
* providing opportunities for self-enhancement,
* increasing concern for others, and
* decreasing ethnic conflict and hate crimes.

Leaders benefit from participating in a program that educates them in characteristics beyond the individual skills of a leader. They benefit from a program that focuses on experiences that provide a more comprehensive understanding of citizenship and create a culture for civic engagement. Community leadership development programs improve the participants' knowledge of community issues and connect them with other like-minded community leaders.

The focus of community leadership development programs is to provide opportunities for participants to engage in new experiences that have meaning for them and to provide support for individuals to collaboratively seek solutions. In chapter four, we mentioned Kolb's experiential learning theory, which states that learning is a continual process and that we learn by doing. The experiential learning cycle demonstrates the never-ending possibilities for individuals to learn, and taking part in new experiences is the critical component of both the community leadership development program and cultivating your relatability.

Such leadership development programs offer a curriculum designed around the community and for leaders who serve their communities. Through these community leadership development programs, participants are encouraged to become more involved with their community, and participants are immersed in the challenges facing their community through hands-on experiences.

In June 2018, sociology professor Hyoung-Yong Kim conducted a study to determine the impact of social capital on community development among fifty-two communities around the United States with more than 20,000 participants, where social capital "refers to the individual and collective resources that can be mobilized through social relations."[3] The results showed social capital contributed to the development of cohesive communities where individuals "act as a unit to deal effectively with problems and challenges."[4]

In the 1970s, psychologist Albert Bandura coined the term *collective efficacy* to explain the way groups of individuals bind together and act as a team. Communities with more collective efficacy experience fewer incivilities. And through community leadership development programs, local networks of community members form and lead to a climate where more people are willing to work toward a common goal. In 2005, community engagement experts Scott Wituk, Sarah Ealey, Mary Jo Clark, and Pat Heiny reported that each year over 750 community leadership development programs across the United States graduate thousands of participants who work in the private, government, and nonprofit industries, as well as other community residents.[5]

Through an interpretive case study analysis, community development experts Wilson Majee, Scott Long, and Deena Smith explored the impact of a community leadership development program. They found participants not only increased their understanding of civic responsibility and awareness of local resources, but also created networking opportunities through interacting with professionals and other community members during and after the program.[6]

Public policy professor Cecilia Ayón and social work professor Cheryl D. Lee conducted a mixed-methods study where they evaluated a six-month-long neighborhood leadership program funded by a city in Southern California. The program invited participants who were already leaders but may not have been aware of city- and community-based resources. The results indicated that alumni of the program were active in their communities in three ways: they "enhanced participation in groups or organizations, increased involvement in a community project or creation of a neighborhood program, and personal growth."[7]

Individuals who have participated in a formal community leadership development program tended to become more involved in their communities, with the biggest impact occurring when programs focusing on knowledge and awareness of the community recruited participants who were not already engaged. When community leadership development programs function successfully, three key components are addressed:

1. Cooperative change through dialogue
2. Collective empowerment
3. Connective leadership

These programs emphasize collaborative relationships among leaders. And relatable leaders understand the importance of supporting programs that help foster new relationships among existing and emerging leaders within a community. Redlands Christian Migrant Association community relations manager and Leadership Collier class of 2022 graduate Gloria Padilla believes "it doesn't take a village to teach a child, but a community that cares enough to be the difference and teach the village."[8]

Graduates of such programs have an improved understanding of their local community, learn how to identify problems in the community, and have the networking in place to become effective leaders in their communities. By encouraging collaboration and shared experiences, successful community leadership development programs empower their participants and alumni to take actions that lead to positive change in communities. And by establishing a program that provides an eye-opening, behind-the-scenes experience for community leaders, the participants gain valuable experiences that further their personal and professional growth.

In discussing how community leadership development programs help create more effective leaders, Beights makes a great point that "the more a leader knows the intricate details of community successes, challenges, and needs, the more effectively leaders can work collaboratively to truly make a difference."[9]

Through her role with the Leadership Collier Foundation, Beights has had the pleasure and honor of seeing and working with dozens, if not hundreds, of leaders whom she respects. She's convinced community leadership development programs are "magnets for bringing together inspirational people,"[10] and her understanding of what it means to be a leader continues to grow based on her experiences with each of these individuals. As a former foster parent, she enjoys chairing a foster family recruitment committee, and she volunteers her time by sitting on half a dozen boards.

As you look at the bigger picture and see how you fit within the whole system of your life, you're taking responsibility for everything you do and how you care for those around you. When you're able to view your community through the lens of many different industries, your worldview changes. Learning about your community and other communities shows you how to relate with a wide variety of people.

Alumni who have attended community leadership development programs mention as one key takeaway the eye-opening experience even when they've spent years or decades within the community. In a series of anonymous interviews, alumni from Leadership Collier reported an increased awareness of social justice, multicultural competence, and civic engagement as a result of their participation in the program. Through Leadership Collier, the participants

* attended learning events that produced emotional experiences for them,
* observed improved interpersonal and intrapersonal skills,
* recognized the importance of value-added contributions, and
* focused on authentic leadership and informed involvement.

Many participants credit their workplace as the catalyst for applying to Leadership Collier, and that means existing leaders play a significant role in determining who has leadership potential not only in their organization, but also within the community. The alumni who were interviewed admitted to an increase in confidence, which also led to increased positive engagement with others both within their organizations and within the community. The in-depth, hands-on curriculum ensured that participants in Leadership Collier learned through new experiences during each session, even when they thought they were already familiar with their community. Getting a behind-the-scenes view of the different challenges facing the community leaders helped further the participants' decisions about when, where, and how to become more involved as leaders within all aspects of their communities.

Leadership Collier acted as a springboard for diving deeper into their community involvement in ways that matter to them as individuals as well as to the community. The alumni recognized ways in which their everyday activities reflected their leadership mentality. Their active involvement in the community stemmed from both a personal interest in the issue and a professional capacity to gather the necessary people to work on a solution.

Even though the need for community leadership development programs is well documented, community leadership development programs report several challenges, such as

* raising funds,
* recruiting members,
* increasing alumni involvement,
* increasing community involvement,
* ensuring diversity,
* having time,
* hiring staff, and
* attracting volunteers.

According to education professor Tarek Azzam and leadership and organization professor Ronald E. Riggio, the top three key challenges are funding, recruiting, and diversity.[11] Many programs rely on mixed modes of funding to operate the program. When a community has a small population or one that is homogenous, recruiting enough participants and creating a diverse and balanced class becomes problematic. The continued pipeline of emerging leaders depends on the existing leaders of regional organizations recognizing in what ways community leadership development programs reduce the gap between leadership development and community development. Relatable leaders support the invaluable role community leadership development programs play in cultivating leaders with competencies and resources necessary to affect positive change in their communities.

Exposing leaders and emerging leaders to a diversity of viewpoints and value systems through an action learning approach is one key component of building leadership capacity. Through continuing education, leaders can enhance their leadership abilities, share perspectives on relevant issues, and work toward solutions in the public interest. When Marisa was first approached by two Leadership Collier alumni to apply for the program, she took her time considering how she would add value by being a participant and not just take up someone else's spot in the class. She understood the value of giving back. We already were attending charity events, but in October of 2020, Collier County launched a foam recycling initiative that caught her attention. The director for Collier County Solid & Hazardous Waste Management Division said, "this is a project the community has wanted."[12] Coming from the community showed Marisa how leadership is not hierarchical and how it focused on sustainable value within her community.

SUSTAINABLE VALUE

Understanding the way sustainable value connects the environment with economic and social issues plays an important part in your development as a relatable leader, especially given that leadership is nonhierarchical. While many companies engage in environmental sustainability practices, there is no universal definition of what environmental sustainability really means for the general population.

John Morelli, professor emeritus of civil engineering technology, environmental management, and safety, explored the needs and problems of sustainability through the assessment of various government and company policies, and developed a universal definition.[13] He proposed that environmental sustainability should be defined as "meeting the resource and services needs of current and future generations without compromising the health of the ecosystems that provide them . . . as a condition of balance, resilience, and interconnectedness that allows human society to satisfy its needs while neither exceeding the capacity of its supporting ecosystems to continue to regenerate the services necessary to meet those needs nor by our actions diminishing biological diversity."[14]

This definition helps relatable leaders better understand what environmental sustainability really entails. Relatable leaders can use the definition to determine whether concerns such as access to key services, awareness of social responsibility, sense of community ownership, or citizen participation are considered when claims are made by companies that their actions have achieved environmental sustainability.

Relatable leaders focus on how their actions and the actions within their communities and organizations impact the world, and this impact demonstrates the importance of balance. Sustainability focuses on long-term effects, and embedding sustainability into your life is a key trait of relatable leaders. Relatable leaders understand how they, and their actions, fit within the entire system, and they transcend their organization and even industry to become beacons throughout the community.

This level of relatable leadership takes time and commitment to achieve, but it's also where societal and environmental innovations are born and implemented. For example, many years ago, after Marisa started teaching seventh graders, she started collecting the tops of aluminum cans. When I asked her why, she said another teacher at the school started an initiative to collect the pop tabs for Ronald McDonald House Charities. That teacher wasn't a superintendent, a principal, or on the school board, so she wasn't a school leader in the hierarchical sense. But she still initiated a program, demonstrating how relatable leaders view leadership as nonhierarchical. By not waiting for someone higher up the organizational chart to propose this initiative, the teacher was able to create a program that added sustainable value to the school's community through recycling and donating to a charity.

Patagonia founder Yvon Chouinard is quoted as saying, "It's not the attainment of the summit. It's the style of the climb." How are you getting to where you're going? Relatable leaders, regardless of where they are within their organization, consider in what ways their everyday actions and use of products impact the environment and society. Patagonia is known for its focus on minimizing their environmental impact and improving its social practices. On Black Friday in 2011, its "Don't Buy This Jacket" full-page ad in the *New York Times* spotlighted the company's values.

Developing a sustainable mindset can start with anyone within an organization, but relatable leaders also need to know what is sustainable on a larger scale. In what other ways should relatable leaders correlate their lives to sustainable value? Organizations can't use and reuse indefinitely without depleting the resources available at the moment. When you take more than you give, you run out, and the larger your organization grows, the more that organization will need to take to sustain itself until it becomes unsustainable. This is the tragedy of commons, and relatable leaders are sensitive to this point.

THE TRAGEDY OF COMMONS

"The tragedy of commons refers to a situation in which individuals with access to a shared resource (also called a common) act in their own interest and, in doing so, ultimately deplete the resource."[15]

One example of the tragedy of commons is traffic congestion. The shared resource is the roads, and individuals act in their own interest by choosing the roads that help them get to where they're going with key factors in mind: less use of gas or quickest way to get there. Traffic congestion usually happens during rush hour when people are going to work. One suggestion to solve this issue is to charge a toll during rush hour. This might have drivers considering alternative paths to get to work, decreasing traffic and putting less stress on the high-traveled road.

When I was the associate dean at a midsize university and an executive director of a technology institute, I faced several environmental and social issues that helped me reframe how to conceptualize certain solutions. Tolls may motivate individuals through monetary penalties, but what if the congestion issue could be addressed through incentives? When individuals take into consideration ways to help the community and the environment, then they are embracing the nonhierarchical aspect of relatable leadership.

Pollution is one of the key factors that impact both the health of individuals and the earth's environmental system. Numerous studies have provided evidence that pollution is devastating to the health and well-being of individuals, including being linked to acute cardiovascular diseases. Pollution is also linked to low birth rate, central nervous system disease, and lung cancer.

I believed that in my roles as associate dean and executive director, I could help move our institute toward becoming more socially and environmentally responsible by focusing on minimizing and eradicating pollution. To address this goal, I crafted the following proposed actions:

* Worked with current administration to limit on-ground course offerings and instead leverage current systems to deliver virtual classes. This limited the need for commuting by students and staff to our main campus.
* Focused on redesigning on-site class meetings to leverage virtual labs and the learning management system.
* Worked with the current administration to reposition our marketing campaigns toward students interested in online programs.
* Worked on refocusing and launching fully online programs, which would lead to the reduction of carbon dioxide.

These strategies helped reduce pollution by implementing telecommuting practices so the institute's students could attend online classes while staff worked remotely more frequently. Telecommuting isn't a new idea, but pollution is an existing problem. Using an interactive design helped the university and the institute become an environmentally responsible and sustainable organization.

Whether it's recycling or saving the tabs of aluminum cans, relatable leaders set an example for how they treat and care for their community and its resources.

CHAPTER EIGHT REFLECTION

In this chapter's reflection, we'd like you to consider how relatable leaders view leadership as nonhierarchical. Nonhierarchical leadership decentralizes responsibilities and instills a sense of commitment to growth and community. Through community leadership development programs, we can gain a greater understanding of how to become effective leaders within our communities and embed sustainability into our lives.

The following questions are designed to help you consider ways to develop a nonhierarchical leadership mindset:

- Who do you consider a leader in your life right now?
- Who do you know is a leader but lacks a traditional leadership title?
- Who are your community leaders but are not elected officials?
- Does your community offer a community leadership development program?
- Do you know anyone who has graduated from a community leadership development program?
- What are some environmental or social issues that matter to you?

Now complete this phrase out loud or in the silence of your mind, and write it down:

I will promote nonhierarchical leadership in the following ways . . .

PART THREE
There Is No Box

In part three, we begin with the concept that you are the CEO of your life, and now it's time to assess your company—Your Life. In this final part of the book, you'll spotlight your strengths and look at other areas of your life where you might need more support. As you work to reframe each and every interaction, becoming a relatable leader might not be easy. This shift in your mindset won't happen overnight, but most leaders aren't looking for a quick fix. You've always been in charge of your own life, but you might not have realized it or been ready to act until now.

In these final chapters, we'll address the concept that there is no box, there is not just one path to get to where you want to go. But you can develop a plan to help you discover ways to increase your influence by cultivating your relatability. By using project management concepts and examples and exercises on how to develop your unique leadership development plan, you'll be able to create your own path to becoming a relatable leader. This is your journey, singular to you, and we hope that you embrace the journey.

9 The Project Management Mindset

When we plan, a common strategy is to write down steps to achieve that plan. Our plans have a similar structure as a train that makes stops along a set path to get from point A to point B. However, trains have tracks that run forward and backward. They are not flexible in direction. They can't adjust easily, and they certainly don't move side to side. One train car can't pass another, and the whole analogy is riddled with reasons why life that moves like a train doesn't work well.

By shifting our perspective to the project management mindset, we turn the train into five separate 18-wheelers. Unlike five cars of one train connected and dependent on each other, the five separate 18-wheelers are able to move beside, behind, in front of, and around each other, allowing us to assess each truck moving forward individually. We set those trucks on a paved highway, and they maintain their forward momentum. If one truck experiences issues, the other ones can move around it. They have the flexibility and agility to speed up and slow down when the timing fits the situation. Imagine the five trucks as the five key ways leaders cultivate their relatability:

1. They know their starting lines.
2. They increase their cultural agility.
3. They practice compassionate communication.
4. They embrace the leadership lifestyle.
5. They view leadership as nonhierarchical.

One truck is not dependent on the other, but they all arrive at the same destination—producing a relatable leader. There is no one way to cultivate your relatability, and you can increase your cultural agility at the same time you're recognizing the value of compassionate communication. You don't need to know your starting lines before you can view leadership as nonhierarchical, and embracing the leadership lifestyle is something that can happen at any time in your leadership development journey.

The ability to shift in a nonlinear fashion is the power of the project management mindset. A plan can be derailed by an object on the tracks, but when you approach your plan with a project management mindset, the way you reach the end goal isn't dependent on one set of tracks. If one piece of your plan hits a roadblock, then the whole plan doesn't need to be redrawn, just the one piece that was blocked. Everything else can continue to move forward, and in the end, you'll have completed a successful project.

I didn't realize this until Simon, a project manager by trade, introduced project management principles to me. He saw me struggling to start and complete a million different goals. I knew what I wanted to accomplish, but I didn't have a way to organize how I was going to get there. When he taught me the project management methodology, my whole world shifted. My small goals piled into large goals, and I discovered endless possibilities.

These final chapters are going to use project management principles as a framework for creating your own personalized leadership development plan, with exercises that you can complete on your own timeline. Leadership development is not a one-size-fits-all process, but with guidance informed by a project management mindset, you'll be able to create a plan that will help you achieve your goals.

One helpful project planning approach is backward planning. This is when you start with the end result in mind. Backward planning helps us examine the details of the plan more carefully. If you've ever thought that you needed to leave the house by a certain time to get to an appointment by a certain time, then you've incorporated backward planning into your thought process. Or if you know you have three errands to run and the stores close by 9 PM, you could estimate the time you need to spend in each store and the travel time to get to the stores to come up with when you should start to run your errands.

As you move through these final pages, we'll use the backward planning approach to create a personal leadership development plan. It might feel different from what you're used to, and that's good because we're asking you to shift your perspective and see that there is no box. To do that, you need to look at things from different angles.

We'll start with identifying where you want to be because unless you know where you're going, you won't be able to head in a meaningful direction. Meandering may be fine for some people, but leadership is a choice you work toward with purpose.

In this chapter, we're going to focus on the project management mindset by providing

* an examination of how portfolios, programs, and projects relate to your life,
* an explanation for how goals and experiences correlate,
* examples of portfolios and the benefit of a Gantt chart,
* factors for successfully achieving goals,
* variables for success, and
* a reflection upon what success looks like.

PORTFOLIOS, PROGRAMS, AND PROJECTS

Successful project managers are some of the most relatable leaders because they are trained to complete complex projects on time, within budget, on scope, and in a variety of different settings with diverse teams often assembled from siloed functional areas. They are cultivating their relatability in all five ways with each project they helm. Over the years, I've employed the project management mindset to every aspect of my life, and this has provided me with a way to clearly see the priorities in my life.

In project management, organizations think about projects in terms of portfolios and programs. Projects are part of programs, which are put into portfolios. Project management focuses on the completion of a collection of tasks that will add value to the overall program. Program management focuses on how the projects coordinate to add value to the overall portfolio. And portfolio management focuses on how a group of programs adds value to the overall objectives of the organization.

An organization can have more than one portfolio categorized by its function or theme. All the programs within that category are related, just as all the projects relate to the program. This mindset helps organizations correlate their strategic objectives (goals) with their mission and vision. If a project doesn't add value to a program, and a program doesn't add value to the portfolio, then the leaders need to assess why they would spend time and money on those projects.

Table 2 illustrates how you as the CEO of your life can use project management principles when thinking about the complexities of your life projects:

TABLE 2 Project Management Principles for Your Life

Project Management Principles	Your Life Projects
Company	Your life
Portfolios	Categories in your life
Programs	Goals within each category
Projects	Collection of tasks to accomplish your goals

FIGURE 3. The Project Management Mindset

Company: Your Life

Portfolio: Categories in your life | Portfolio: Categories in your life | Portfolio: Categories in your life

Program: Goals in this category | Program: Goals in this category | Program: Goals in this category

Projects: Tasks to complete this goal | Projects: Tasks to complete this goal | Projects: Tasks to complete this goal

Projects: Tasks to complete this goal

Can have more than one project (collection of tasks to accomplish the goal) under each program.

Can have more than one program (goal) under each portfolio

Program: Goals in this category | Program: Goals in this category | Program: Goals in this category

Your life is your entire organization, and you will have goals throughout your lifetime. By organizing your goals by category, you're creating portfolios. These portfolios separate your goals into different areas of your growth, such as fitness, career, or finances. Like the 18-wheelers, you're able to make progress in each portfolio at different speeds. Your career goals aren't necessarily dependent on your fitness goals, although there is plenty of evidence suggesting a correlation between healthy habits and career success.

Within each portfolio, your goals are the programs. Program management is managing a collection of related projects, so the goals themselves are the programs within each portfolio. These programs are what you want to accomplish within each area of your life, such as completing a 5K, which is in your fitness portfolio. The collection of tasks you need to complete to achieve your goals are the projects. Each program will have a collection of projects that need to be completed in order for you to complete your program. For example, if one of your portfolios is fitness, and a program in your fitness portfolio is running the 5K, then you might have five or so different projects to complete that program, such as budgeting for and buying the right gear, researching and registering for the 5K, and planning and securing any travel arrangements. Projects are temporary, so they have a start and end date, and breaking up the program into a collection of projects with their own small accomplishments leads to large accomplishments when you complete the program.

By viewing your life through portfolios of your goals, you can get a holistic view of everything you want to accomplish. Programs allow you to plan, manage, and execute your goals in a coordinated way that contributes to the success of that portfolio. When you organize those goals (programs) into portfolios, you'll be able to see which areas of your life—family, career, fitness—need more attention and which goals add the most value to your overall life. Whether you sit down and write this out formally, or just have it in your head, you can see how your goals contribute to how you live your life.

When you have too many goals in one portfolio, you might think that your life feels unbalanced. If your goals in another portfolio are too few, you might think that your life is lacking in some area. This mindset ensures you're looking at your life from all angles, and this holistic view will act as a foundation as you cultivate your relatability by including a wide range of experiences within each of your goals.

Charting Your Life's Portfolios

Let's start by writing down what you want to accomplish. Write down all the things you want to do in any order and without thought to anything other than that it's a goal you want to achieve. Your goals are the programs you want to accomplish within each of the portfolios of your life. For this exercise, I'm going to use five, but I encourage you to write down as many as you can think of.

Here are my five example goals:

1. See the sunset at the beach at least once a week for a year.
2. Read one hundred books in a calendar year.
3. Support local businesses during November.
4. Spend time with family and friends over the holidays.
5. Discover a new bottle of red wine by the end of the year.

Next, group these goals into portfolios. You can name the portfolios whatever you'd like. Since goals 3 and 5 help the economy, I'm going to group goals 3 and 5 into a consumer portfolio. Goals 1 and 4 are in my leisure portfolio, leaving goal 2 in my personal development portfolio. Other areas of your life that you might like to categorize are fitness or health, finance, and family. All my portfolios contribute holistically to my life.

In this example, each specific collection of tasks that is needed to accomplish the goals represents an individual project, and a project is a temporary endeavor with set start and end dates. For example, if I want to read one hundred books in a calendar year, that's one program within the personal development portfolio. The projects under that program will focus on each of these books and will include the tasks associated with choosing the book to read, buying the book, and making time for reading the book. Each project will need to be planned, executed, monitored, and evaluated.

Table 3 provides another visual of the analogy. By viewing how the projects relate to the programs and how those programs fit with the portfolios, I'm able to see how each project helps me complete a program, how completing that program contributes to that portfolio, and how that portfolio adds value to my life. If something doesn't fit or doesn't add value to your life, then you can see where adjustments could be made. We'll look at that in the next section.

At a program level, your attention should be focused on managing projects in a coordinated way so your timelines for completing your tasks aren't in conflict with each other. For example, if I want to spend time with my family over the winter holidays, but I also have a goal to visit the Strasbourg Christmas Market, one of those programs would need to be adjusted so that they didn't happen at the same time. You should also focus on the strategic alignment of these projects.

Within My Life, I may always have a personal development portfolio, but the programs and projects within that portfolio may change from year to year or as I complete each program or project. As with the Strasbourg Christmas Market example, by managing these projects in a coordinated way, where I might look at how long the market is running and visit the market at the beginning of the month before traveling to see my family, I will be able to complete both programs without a conflict in scheduling. This is the benefit of program management and looking at the links between programs.

TABLE 3 The Portfolios of My Life

Company: My Life		
Portfolio: Consumer	Portfolio: Leisure	Portfolio: Personal Development
Program: Support local businesses during November Projects (a collection of tasks to accomplish each goal): • Find local businesses by researching area and owners • Plan which day and how much to spend • Visit store and buy items • Discover ways to support local businesses other than by just buying their goods (such as leaving reviews)	Program: See the sunset at the beach at least once a week for a year Projects (a collection of tasks to accomplish each goal): • Choose a beach or beaches • Review sunset times for the beach or beaches • Coordinate travel plans for getting to the beach or beaches	Program: Read one hundred books in one calendar year Projects (a collection of tasks to accomplish each goal): • Choose which books to read • Buy the books • Read the books
Program: Discover a new bottle of red wine by the end of the year Projects (a collection of tasks to accomplish each goal): • Ask family and friends for referrals • Visit wine stores • Research wineries • Visit wineries	Program: Spend time with family and friends over the holidays Projects (a collection of tasks to accomplish each goal): • Choose which holidays • Decide which family and friends • Decide in what format to spend time with them • Make plans while spending time with them	

In contrast, projects are focused on the tactical level, working to create specific deliverables within a scope, a budget, a time frame, and quality level. Since all projects are temporary and have an end date, we should see progress toward our goal as we complete each project.

One key to focus on is to choose goals that add value to the way you want to cultivate your relatability. These goals can and should fall under any of your portfolios, as you cultivate relatability in and for both your personal and professional lives.

When you're establishing your goals, keep in mind how they are adding value to

* knowing your starting lines,
* increasing your cultural agility,
* recognizing the value of compassionate communication,
* embracing the leadership lifestyle, and
* practicing nonhierarchical leadership.

WHY YOU WANT TO ACHIEVE YOUR GOALS

Now that you have your list of goals (programs) organized in such a way that you can see how they contribute to your overall life, it's time to analyze the value you'll achieve by completing those goals. To check if your goals add value to your life, first read each one of them and see if anything can be revised or removed. A goal to buy a new car can be revised to a goal to buy a four-door sedan with a 50,000-mile warranty. By being specific, you're removing any vagueness that could distract you from what you really mean to accomplish.

Next, check your goals to see if you need to add something that's missing. Sometimes as you're rephrasing, you'll remember something else that you'd like to include as a program that will add value to your life. Also, if you see that one portfolio, such as career, has only two goals, you might decide to add two more, to make it more balanced with another portfolio, such as fitness, that might have four. In my example, I have only one program listed to complete under the personal development portfolio, so I would want to add one more to make the portfolios more balanced.

As you read each goal, consider why you want to achieve it. This *why* is your motivation. Why do you want to pursue this goal rather than stay where you are at this moment in life? What will keep you moving forward when you face conflict in your pursuit of this goal? Understanding your motivation will help you focus on your goals when you're faced with a challenge to complete them.

What is stopping you from achieving your goals right now? By identifying any conflicts standing in the way, you can better prepare how you will face those speed bumps. For example, if one program you want to complete is to wake up at five o'clock every morning and stretch, and you know that going to bed too late because you drink coffee in the evenings will make this goal problematic, then you have to decide if drinking coffee in the evenings is worth not achieving your early morning stretching goal. If you find that the obstacles are more than your motivation alone can overcome, then you might consider removing that goal from your list and choosing one that inspires motivation that is strong enough to overcome any challenges.

In order to determine if your goals are adding value to your life, you need a realistic assessment of what it will take to get where you want to go. Author Debra Dixon's book *GMC: Goal, Motivation & Conflict* has offered Marisa helpful building blocks for her writing, and learning them from her, I've adapted GMC to planning a road map for leadership development. By listing your goal, your motivation, and any conflicts, you can review each goal and decide whether or not you'd like to keep that goal in your portfolio.

Table 4 is an example of how you can keep track of your goals, motivations, and potential conflicts.

TABLE 4 GMC Example

Goal	To read one hundred books by the end of the year
Motivation	To learn new things, expand my thinking, support authors, and help me increase my cultural agility
Conflict	Not having enough time, being pulled in too many directions, being interrupted while reading, and not being able to find the books I want to read

TABLE 5 Blank GMC Table

Goal	
Motivation	
Conflict	

Consider your goals and complete Table 5 to help you reflect on the relevance and priority of your goals. Because we only get a finite amount of time on this planet, knowing your motivations for your goals will help you put them into perspective. Once you have a clean list of your goals, you can begin to write down each project that needs to be completed to achieve that goal. For example, under my goal to read one hundred books by the end of the year, I have three projects listed:

1. Choose which books to read
2. Buy books
3. Read books

For every project within this goal, a host of tasks are needed to be completed. When I'm choosing which books to read, I will make a concentrated effort to research a variety of genres and authors before I decide on the criteria for assessing each book. Then I'll research several different venues where I could purchase the books and analyze the best one to pick. If I choose a small local business during the month of November, I'll also achieve a goal in my consumer portfolio.

EXPERIENTIAL LEARNING

Having goals and being able to review them and provide a rationale for why those goals matter is critical to anyone's development. But to increase your relatability alongside your leadership development, you need to add another layer—experiences. The road to achieving each goal includes a wide range of experiences to help you learn and grow. Recall Kolb's experiential learning cycle from chapter 4. When we experience something, we either think about it, thus creating a memory, or we forget about it. This stage of reflecting allows us to critically assess the experience and learn from it so that we can use that experience to act on new experiences.

Having diverse experiences gives you a broader frame of reference for when you're dealing with new situations. A leader who has faced one hundred different scenarios will have a better chance of successfully navigating new scenarios as a result of combining the lessons learned from all previous one hundred experiences. This leader has an edge over leaders who have experienced far fewer situations that were similar in nature. Stephen M. R. Covey, author of

The SPEED of Trust, wrote, "So they're working in a company—maybe they've been there for ten or fifteen years—but instead of having fifteen years of experience, they really only have one year of experience fifteen times!"[1]

Focus on creating different experiences to help you align your goals with experiences that will further your growth. Start by determining who you are as a learner and leader. What previous knowledge do you have about leaders and leadership? What personal experiences do you have that influences your beliefs about leaders and leadership?

We've described relatable leaders as being authentic, inspiring, serving, and transformational. What aspiring experiences could you add to your list that would help you enhance these attributes in yourself? These experiences should include

* situations in which you're interacting with people who are not like you and
* situations in which you can learn by doing something you've not yet had the chance to do.

These aspiring experiences are your goals. Since we're using project management as our frame, we suggest using a Gantt chart—a visual chronological representation of a project from start to finish. By creating a Gantt chart, as detailed or as brief as you'd like, you'll be able to measure your progress. At a minimum, we suggest including a start date, an end date, an approximate number of experiences, and a weekly experiences goal on your chart. Even though cultivating your relatability will take time, you can start right now, so consider making your start date today. Then give yourself an achievable amount of time to plug in at least ten experiences.

Table 6 is an example of what the first few months might look like for you as you plan experiences that will help cultivate your relatability.

TABLE 6 Experiences Example in a Gantt Chart

Experiences	Length of Time (Weeks)											
	1	2	3	4	5	6	7	8	9	10	11	12
Motivate someone on your team	▓	▓	▓	▓								
Practice self-compassion by not criticizing yourself	▓	▓	▓	▓								
Volunteer to chair or help at an event		▓	▓	▓								
Purposefully look at conflicts without assigning a right or wrong or good or bad label	▓	▓	▓	▓	▓							
Learn a new technical skill in another area at work					▓	▓	▓	▓				
Take a conflict resolution course					▓	▓	▓					
Sit on a board for a year or more						▓	▓	▓	▓	▓	▓	▓

Table 7 is an example of a twelve-week blank Gantt chart. Each experience is a goal, so as you're revising and adjusting your portfolios, consider where and how each of the experiences you incorporate fit within the holistic view of your life.

TABLE 7 Blank Gantt Chart

Length of Time (Weeks)											
Experiences	1	2	3	4	5	6	7	8	9	10	11	12

CRITICAL SUCCESS FACTORS

There is nothing holding you back but you. Optimists believe that with the right amount of effort, we can achieve almost anything. Henry Ford is quoted as saying, "Whether you think you can, or you think you can't—you're right." I've found this to be true on too many occasions to discount it—our attitude makes a difference in our success. In addition to our attitude, there are other key factors that contribute to our success. In project management, these are called critical success factors (CSFs), and they apply to our goals as well.

We can draft our goals, check them to make sure we have enough motivation to overcome any conflict, and revise them to include experiences that will cultivate our relatability. These are gigantic steps toward shaping our unique path to becoming a relatable leader. But CSFs must go right for us to succeed. Just as the project manager is the leader who must thoroughly understand the entire project—including risks, issues, and actions to be taken—so, too, must you, the CEO of your life, understand all facets of your development program. In other words, you are responsible and accountable for leading all aspects of every stage of your life.

When we apply that mindset to our own leadership development, it means that we—as the CEO—must thoroughly understand

* what we want to accomplish and
* that we are responsible and accountable for every stage of achieving that accomplishment.

Before we create our own personalized leadership development plan, looking at our CSFs will help best prepare us when designing our desired outcomes.

There are ten CSFs that contribute to project success.[2] As you review these CSFs, consider how they apply to your goals. You might think about how these ten CSFs contributed to the outcome of a short-term goal you've already met or how they apply to an ongoing endeavor you're currently pursuing.

1. **Project mission.** Initial clarity of goals and general directions.
2. **Top management support.** Willingness of top management to provide the necessary resources, authority, and power for project success.
3. **Project schedule and plans.** Detailed specification of the individual action steps required for project implementation.
4. **Client consultation.** Communication among all impacted parties.
5. **Personnel.** Recruitment, selection, and training of the necessary personnel for the project team.
6. **Technical tasks.** Availability of the required technology and expertise to accomplish the specific technical action steps.
7. **Client acceptance.** Selling the final project to its ultimate intended users.
8. **Monitoring and feedback.** Timely provision of comprehensive control information at each phase in the implementation process.
9. **Communication.** Provision of an appropriate network and necessary data for all key factors in the project implementation
10. **Troubleshooting.** Ability to handle unexpected crises and deviations from plan.

If we look at these ten CSFs in relation to our own leadership development, we can see how we might be dependent on others to reach some of our goals successfully. In addition to these ten CSFs, four additional factors[3] beyond our control are considered external factors. These external factors can impact success in attaining a goal or completing a project.

1. **Characteristics of the project team leader.** Competence of the project leader (administratively, interpersonally, and technically) and the amount of authority available to perform their duties.

2. **Power and politics.** Degree of political activity within the organization and perception of the project as furthering an organization member's self-interests.

3. **Environmental events.** External organizational or environmental factors impacting the operations of the project team, either positively or negatively.

4. **Urgency.** Perception of the importance of the project or the need to implement the project as soon as possible.

PATTERNS FROM SUCCESS FACTORS

By examining the CSFs in relation to our own goals, we can see how likely we are to accomplish those goals on scope, on time, and on budget. We can also review why we want to achieve each goal and evaluate how achieving each goal contributes to the overall betterment of our life. If we continue to examine our motivation behind our goal, we will be better able to focus throughout the time it takes us to achieve that goal. Additionally, by keeping track of our goals through the use of a Gantt chart, we can see if we're on time or behind schedule. As we continue to develop our leadership style, we're also increasing our chances of successfully completing our current and future goals.

As you continue to create new goals, you'll be able to determine where they fit on your timeline and how they align with other goals you're currently pursuing. Not all of your goals will seem urgent, and you can remove the ones that don't seem necessary. That way, the only goals you're working toward are the ones that are a priority over other distractions in your life.

PROJECT SUCCESS VARIABLES

Just as in project management where certain variables can help us predict if a project will be successful, so, too, can project success variables help us determine if we will meet our goals. The project manager has certain authority and accountability and needs to exhibit reliability and responsibility for the success of a project, just as you do with your goals. As you read through the project success variables that can be measured by the actions of a project manager, consider how these success variables also apply to yourself as a CEO and how they apply to your current leaders or supervisors in your professional career. Remember, in my example the projects are the tasks needed to complete your goals.

The following is a list of project success variables:

* Have a clear understanding of the project's and the organization's strategic goals.
* Be reliable.
* Develop realistic cost, schedule, performance, and value goals.
* Develop and maintain backup plans for potential problems.
* Organize a flexible structure of reporting with the right mixture of authority and accountability.
* Leverage existing processes.
* Use all possible project management tools.
* Be results oriented.
* Understand and manage risks.
* Design well-defined requirements and specifications.
* Understand the scope of the project and keep that scope in mind throughout project execution.

* Have realistic expectations and time frame.
* Institute, evaluate, measure, and achieve clear performance metrics.
* Always think of value adds for projects.
* Focus on performance measures.
* Control all six success factors during project execution: scope and scope creep, schedule, budget and cost, resources, performance, and value.

MEASUREMENT OF SUCCESS VARIABLES

Organizational commitment, especially commitment from top management, is a critical factor in project success. The same is true of your leadership development. Your commitment to your own development is critical to its success. You display this commitment by ensuring the completion of the project, solving problems as they arise, supporting the cost of the project, and being the spokesperson for the relevance of the project in relation to the success of the portfolio. As the portfolio manager, program manager, and project manager, you need to act with responsibility and reliability toward each project's success.

The following is a list of ways to gauge the level of success you may achieve:

* Have a clear understanding of the strategic goals of the project and the organization.
* Provide adequate training and education.
* Adapt to change.
* Align project strategy to organizational strategy.
* Communicate accurately.
* Show enthusiasm for and commitment to the project.
* Be realistic regarding schedules.
* Have a realistic budget in mind.

* Understand the scope of the project.
* Be optimistic but avoid overoptimism.
* Allow plenty of time for planning.
* Be accountable.
* Manage processes.
* Have a clear vision of projects and deadlines.

PHENOMENA OF SUCCESS

With all this knowledge of patterns, variables, and factors for success, why aren't we learning any lessons? Why do 75 percent of projects still pass through a troubled phase in need of recovery? Why do project managers consistently deal with off-schedule, off-budget, off-scope projects, even given the vast number of resources, certifications, and best practices offered?

Why do some of our goals remain unfilled?

Management.

I use the term *management* deliberately here. After over twenty years in the industry, I've come to differentiate between a management team and a leadership team. But that's a different book. We can't boil the ocean in this one. For now, I posit these questions to you:

* What kind of CEO of your life do you want to be?
* Which traits will seep from your pores and reveal your most authentic self?

By setting small goals that will pile into large goals and produce endless possibilities, you will erase the lines you've drawn around yourself. Those lines include any labels and boundaries you've given yourself that are keeping you from becoming your best leader self.

CHAPTER NINE REFLECTION

Success means different things to different people. What one person wants to accomplish may seem insignificant to another. As we plan our path to becoming a relatable leader, using the project manager mindset can help us focus on achieving our goals by offering visuals to clarify how each component of our life lines up with our overall idea of what success means to us. We can see how our life has different categories (portfolios) and within those categories we have goals (programs). In order to complete those programs, we have a collection of tasks (projects).

In this chapter's reflection, we'd like you to think about the following questions as they relate to your life:

- What are the important portfolios in your life?
- What programs are part of these portfolios?
- What projects do you need to complete within these programs?
- What CSFs resonated most with you?
- What are your measurements of success?

Now complete this phrase out loud or in the silence of your mind, and write it down:

I'll consider myself a success when I've . . .

10 Values and Vision

Who is John Galt?

In Ayn Rand's *Atlas Shrugged*, Dagny is the fierce female executive who goes after what she wants without reservation and despite constant opposition. She has goals, just as you created and revised goals for yourself in the previous chapter. And she faced obstacles, just like you will. But through it all, she never lost sight of who she was or how she thought the world around her should be. Now it's time to look at the next part of your leadership development: values and vision.

Meghan Casserly, Forbes staff, lays out in perfection "Ten Lessons from Dagny Taggart":[1]

1. Ignore the haters.
2. Don't argue, just do.
3. Don't let a man boss you around—unless, of course, you like it.
4. Praise good work.
5. Go with your gut.

6. Don't let your ego get the best of you.
7. Beauty is a weapon—especially when battling other women.
8. Don't walk around when you can cut straight across.
9. Don't threaten to do something unless you can follow through.
10. Just do you.

These lessons are powerful and, in many cases, self-explanatory. Emerging leaders are already figuring out how to follow this advice. In this chapter, we want to explore the last lesson: just do you.

Finding out who we are and how we fit into all of the complex systems we are a part of can be challenging for even the most put-together leader. It can be exhausting trying to achieve that elusive balance among all those expectations placed upon you—real or imagined—by yourself or by others, by people you know and love, and by people you don't know and have never met and who may pass you in the street and judge you anyway. We feel it's vital for emerging leaders navigating their growth holistically to take some time to embrace the fact that there is no box because you are you, and you're the only one of you who can lead the way you do.

But what does *just do you* look like? As the CEO of your life, you are your most critical success factor. There will be many factors you cannot control, but you can control what you do.

In this chapter, we're going to focus on your values and vision by providing

* guidance for how you define yourself,
* a discussion about how your values shape your vision,
* an introduction to personality assessments and leadership influence styles,
* ways to write your vision statement, and
* a reflection upon your values and vision.

DEFINING YOU

Before anyone can reach their full leadership potential, they must know who they are. In author Stedman Graham's book *Identity Leadership*, he states, "It all hinges on how you define yourself and who determines that definition: you or someone else."[2] There are plenty of exercises that can help us uncover who we are, and in defining ourselves, it's also important to reflect upon how others see us. We may fight against all the labels that help define us to others, but labels exist because they're a good place to find common ground with others, and, after all, we've been guiding you toward becoming a relatable leader this whole time.

This is a good moment to write down all the titles that describe the roles you fill for everyone else in your life.

Here's a starter list:

Wife   Daughter   Father   Mother   Grandparent   Cousin
Husband   Son   Brother   Sister   Nephew   Niece
Professor   Author   Director   Leader   Project manager
Coach   Mentor   Cheerleader   Friend   Change agent

These labels work in subtle and not so subtle ways to categorize us according to how we relate to others. We might behave a certain way with one group to fit the expectation of the title. Perhaps you adjust your vocabulary or tone one way when meeting with your boss and another way when talking with your friends. That doesn't mean you're being inauthentic in either of those situations. In fact, if you can slip into the different roles with ease and still feel like yourself, then that's your relatability at work.

These labels don't make up the whole of who we are. They are just the frames surrounding us that stack up over time. The whole process of becoming a relatable leader is to become comfortable in a wide range of contexts, and the more situations you're able to encounter with ease, the more relatable you are. Now's a great time to think about who you are beyond all those roles and titles. What does *just do you* look like?

When you take away all the other titles and what those titles imply, who are you? This links back to the Who You Want to Be section in chapter four. At this point, you're looking for links between your personal and professional personalities, and you do that through establishing your values. Your values define you more than any title or label. If you find yourself in a place where your values don't align with your labels, then you lose your ability to become your best self. When you live your values, you're taking ownership of your life.

DEFINING VALUES

A value is a person's principles or standards of behavior, one's judgment of what is important in life.[3]

CHOOSE YOUR VALUES

In *The Confidence Gap*, medical practitioner, psychotherapist, and life coach Russ Harris says that values are more important than goals. You choose your values, but you might not achieve your goals. Because of this, Harris states: "True success is living by your values."[4]

Just as leadership is a choice, so, too, is choosing your core values. We all have a different starting line, and we are a mosaic of the bits and pieces of others who have influenced our lives from birth until right now. In order to break down those boundaries—self-imposed or otherwise—to become our best leader self, we must align our lifestyle with our leadership style, and that starts with stating our core values. These values are the framework we use to make all the decisions in our lives. Maybe you already know what your core values are, and that's fantastic. But what if you don't? How can you identify what you value?

One fairly universal concept is that we often most appreciate someone or something once they are gone. What we cherish reflects what we value. We're no longer surprised when someone says they're swamped or overwhelmed, because so many people we've met don't value their time. Time is our most precious commodity in our limited and unpredictable time on Earth, and yet we give our time to people, causes, and activities that might not align with our values. So we suggest you start there—with how you spend your time—as you narrow down your core values.

Here are some example values to help you get started identifying yours:

* Authenticity
* Adventure
* Autonomy
* Balance
* Compassion
* Community
* Competency
* Creativity
* Cultural agility
* Curiosity
* Entrepreneurship
* Ethical behavior
* Flexibility
* Friendships

* Happiness
* Humor
* Integrity
* Justice
* Kindness
* Knowledge
* Leadership
* Learning
* Love
* Open-mindedness
* Optimism
* Respect
* Social justice
* Trust

THREE WAYS TO FIGURE OUT YOUR VALUES

1. **Write down all the values you can think of.** The longer the list, the better. If you want to use the list above to help you brainstorm, that's great. From your list, circle five to ten values that most resonate with you.

2. **Think about the people you spend the most time with.** Write down their names and the approximate number of hours each person is in your immediate radius.

3. **Look at the values you circled and the people with whom you spend the most time.** In your opinion, do these people share the values you circled? Anyone who doesn't match your list of values is not helping you live your values.

The values that resonate with you and match the people who spend the most time with you are the core values you are living by right now. If the list looks complete to you, then give yourself a high five! If you're missing a value you wish was there, brainstorm ways you can engage with people who embrace that value so you integrate it into your life.

In her blog, life coach and empowerment speaker Ritu Bhasin suggests taking a few moments each day to write down three things that made you feel good, made you feel bad, made you feel useful, others did that you admired, and others did that you disliked. The themes, experiences, and behaviors illustrate how your values show up throughout your day.

If your goal is to become a better leader and you want to live by your values, then the challenge becomes balancing being you with being relatable. As an imperfect human, you may not always make choices based on your core values, but as you cultivate your relatability, you'll continue the ongoing process of learning how to become a more relatable leader while remaining true to your values.

PERSONAL VERSUS PROFESSIONAL PERSONALITY

Over the years, I've taken personality tests, and the results have changed over time. I'm convinced this is because of the environment within which I was functioning. Your personality shouldn't have to change between your personal and professional environments. The way you act in one place should be the same as you act in another place, and your core values and preferences should remain the same even when you're on vacation. What does this mean? It means you don't have to pretend. Anywhere. Because when you're living your most authentic life, you're embracing the leadership lifestyle. Leading the leadership lifestyle is equivalent to merging your personal and professional personalities.

If you haven't heard of the Myers-Briggs Type Indicator personality assessment, I suggest you look it up. Having completed the assessment at various points over the years, I've noticed how the way I answer each question is influenced by my age at the time, my current job, the time of day, and other outstanding factors. I've found that depending on when (in their career) a person might take the assessment, the results may vary.

Once I merged my personal and professional personalities, my scores became more consistent over time. I found the results fascinating and applicable to learning more about my personality and how it was influenced by my professional position when I wasn't leading a leadership lifestyle. I remember one particular job where I acted one way at work that went against my instinctual way of behaving, and this flipping back and forth was exhausting. My boss not only asked me to behave in a manner contradictory to how I believed people in an office should behave, but the actual job duties I needed to perform to be considered successful by management were not in alignment with what I enjoyed doing. If I learned anything from my time in that office, it was the importance of knowing my personality and being able to maintain an authentic personality in my personal and professional life.

In the Ethical Leadership course I teach at Georgetown University, my students and I explore the six major factors that make up a person's personality using the HEXACO (Honesty-Humility, Emotionality, eXtraversion, Agreeableness, Conscientiousness, Openness to Experience) model of personality created by psychology professors Michael C. Ashton and Kibeom Lee.[5] This model examines the personality through factors and facets. The six factors are the broad dimensions of the personality that are then distilled into facets, or traits, on a sliding scale of high to low. Studies have shown support for the connection between a person's social and ethical behavior. Because leaders often deal with personalities over products, I've come to believe that a person's character matters more than their competencies.

That's not to say there isn't a time and place for different leadership approaches. We certainly should adjust to the circumstances, accommodating for a growth mode or a recession, for instance. Varied leadership styles are effective for different groups, but when someone has a sense of where they are as a leader and how their personality influences their instinctual leadership tendencies, that's when a person can best match their personality with their natural leadership style within a certain industry.

Table 8 shows the HEXACO six-factor model of personality. The factors show the six dimensions of a person's personality, and the facets are the levels within each of the factors. We are all positioned somewhere on the scale of high to low within each facet. A person who scores high in the organization facet prefers a structured approach and seeks order, so they may thrive in an environment where the office space is tidy rather than haphazard.

If you haven't had a chance to look up the HEXACO Personality Inventory online, we suggest you do so at hexaco.org. If you have, how aligned are the results with who you think you are? Relatedly, how aligned are the results with the type of job you currently hold? As you read through the table, consider your personality and how you're developing as a leader.

TABLE 8 HEXACO Six-Factor Model of Personality

Factors	Facets
Honesty-Humility	Sincerity, fairness, greed avoidance, modesty
Emotionality	Fearfulness, anxiety, dependence, sentimentality
Extraversion	Social self-esteem, social boldness, sociability, liveliness
Agreeableness	Forgiveness, gentleness, flexibility, patience
Conscientiousness	Organization, diligence, perfectionism, prudence
Openness to experience	Aesthetic appreciation, inquisitiveness, creativity, unconventionality

Why use this model to assess your personality? Because everyone can see themselves in varying degrees within each of the facets, and by understanding that we all have some level of each of these aspects to our personality, we are able to better understand how others also fall within a range. It's not one or the other. A person isn't sincere or not sincere. Everyone has some level of sincerity; it just depends on how much, and this circles back to a person's positionality.

In many complex situations, many leaders will find it challenging to get an entire team 100 percent on board with something. Because leaders manage personalities more than products, managing emotions is a critical component of leadership.

Today's society is more globalized than ever before, and understanding your personality as well as the personalities of those around you is critical for your success as a leader. Our personalities reveal so much about who we are. By understanding how our personalities fit within society, within our work space, and within our family, we can see how best to align our leadership style to our lifestyle.

INFLUENCING STYLE

It's important to know how a person's personality can match their natural leadership style, but we should also be aware that sometimes different leadership styles may need to be engaged to reach a desired outcome.

Identifying your primary influencing style is the first step toward improving your ability to motivate others. Once you have identified your style, it should be easier to notice others' influencing styles. Building awareness of your own and others' influencing styles can help you detect when your approach isn't working and then change how you're approaching a particular situation. Being able to read a situation and adjust your communication style is a powerful skill.

Our style develops as a result of our starting line, our job, and the people we work with. As leaders interested in our leadership development, it's critical to assess our influencing styles through the eyes of others as well, such as our peers, subordinates, and supervisors. We do not see ourselves the same way others see us, and we benefit from introspection, self-analysis, and seeking professional development and personal growth. By self-monitoring, we can increase our emotional intelligence and be more thoughtful in our work with others to encourage and support their best performance.

In a *Harvard Business Review* article titled "What's Your Influencing Style," organizational development experts Chris Musselwhite and Tammie Plouffe reveal that you can improve your powers of communication by learning "to recognize and use each of the five styles" of influence:[6]

1. Rationalizing
2. Asserting
3. Negotiating
4. Inspiring
5. Bridging

By using these styles to identify our inclination to communicate primarily in one particular way, we can also learn to shift with agility among all influencing styles. Being able to identify when others are using influencing styles that differ from our preferred style is critical, because as Musselwhite and Plouffe state, "When we are operating unconsciously out of a preference (our style) and not seeing the results we expect, we actually have a tendency to intensify our preferred behavior—even when it's not working!" But first, we must be able to recognize our primary style, and then we should be able to recognize the influencing styles of others.

Consider the definitions in Table 9 and see if you can identify the style that sounds most like you. Once you've read through the definitions, you can get an idea of what your preferred influencing style is. Then you can think about the people in your life and consider which style they use to influence you and others. This increased awareness of how other people communicate will help you detect when you need to shift into another style to best achieve the results you want.

TABLE 9 The Five Influence Styles

Style	Definition
Rationalizing	Analytical, rational, prefers facts and data to support point of view
Asserting	Confident, straight shooter, challenges the ideas of others
Negotiating	Collaborator, compromiser, seeks harmony and consensus
Inspiring	Encourager, advocator for others' point of view, uses anecdotes and metaphors, creates a sense of a shared mission
Bridging	Mediator, creates relationships and connections, builds coalitions

LIKE A LEADER

During a doctoral course at Northeastern University, leadership professor Harriette Rasmussen posited the following fill-in-the-blank statement to her students. As part of creating your own personal leadership development plan, take a moment to consider this for yourself:

> When I am at my best as a leader, I am like a _____.

Here is an example of how to fill this blank:

> When I am at my best as a leader, I am like a compass.
> The best version of my leader self is when I'm guiding others
> along unique paths, helping them erase lines, and explore
> unknown territory toward becoming positive change agents.
> Marisa Cleveland

Whatever description you use in place of a compass, it should represent the type of leader you want to be and how you want others to perceive you as a leader. This is the quality you want your experiences to lead you to, and this is the quality your lifestyle and leadership style should share harmoniously. Once you identify the best version of yourself, your work doesn't stop there. Discovering what success looks like for you and uncovering the type of leader you want to be is only the beginning. To work toward being your best as a leader at all times, you need to develop a leadership vision.

LEADERSHIP VISION

By identifying what you are like when you are at your best as a leader, you've spotlighted how you want others to view you as a leader. If you said you are like a compass, that means you probably want those you influence to see you as a guide. But we don't know how others will perceive us. We can only influence how we want others to see us. We can only behave in a way that gives others the impressions to form opinions of how we are as leaders and as people. As with our reputation, we can't tell people who we are. We show them every day through the way we live, and they form their own opinions about us.

Your vision for yourself is an essential part of developing your leadership style. Over time, this leadership style becomes the consistent expectation that your teams hold when they work with you. If you're all over the place, your team won't really know what to expect from you. So while your leadership style is something you can control by the way you lead, it's also something you can't control, because it's the impression your team has of you based upon how you lead them. As a leader, you're welcoming others into your space, and your vision and mission guide your leadership style. When your vision and mission align, your team will have a clearer understanding of your values, and they will see consistency across what you say, what you do, what others say about you and your work, and all the other unique aspects of your leadership style that make you you. This is just as important as how companies brand themselves through their values. I have worked for many organizations in the past that have displayed their vision and mission statements on their walls for all employees to read so that everyone can see and remind themselves of who the organization is and where it's going. This type of value statement highlights the key principles the organization wants employees to follow in order to achieve their vision through implementing their mission.

Organizations thrive by developing a road map for realizing their vision, and so, too, do relatable leaders. As a result, leaders become adept not only at setting a vision, but also at conducting an organizational diagnosis at the appropriate level to be able to implement meaningful and effective organizational strategies required to achieve that vision. If you can realize your own vision for your life, you'll be able to conduct your own diagnosis to implement meaningful and effective strategies to achieve your vision.

As you're creating your vision statement, consider the changes you may need to make to your life to realize your vision. You may need to address issues and make adjustments necessary to stay on track. Working to solidify a vision and then pursuing the goals and experiences that will enable you to bring that vision to life will ultimately enhance your relatability and help you become an influential force within the world.

Leaders have the potential to improve the human condition. Leaders have the capability of generating enormous amounts of joy and love for life in themselves and in others. Creating your vision statement entails more than answering a simple question—what inspires you? You must also investigate why something inspires you. Just as an organization's vision statement captures how it wants to be known in the world, part of your leadership identity is how you envision yourself and how you want others to see you.

Every leader needs to establish a vision to continually challenge, experiment, and venture outside of their own boundaries in order to grow into a better leader. After establishing a vision, leaders must develop a road map for realizing that vision.

WRITING YOUR VISION STATEMENT

Your vision statement clarifies how you plan to achieve your goals. Vision statements can be written for an individual, a family, a group, or an organization. Your vision statement is a high-concept, future-looking statement that reminds you where you want to be. Vision statements are powerful because they can help you stay focused and guide your direction.

SIMON'S VISION STATEMENT

My vision is to create a world full of relatable leaders for the betterment of society.

Before we dive into drafting your vision statement, let's look at some examples of organizational vision statements:

"Our vision is to create a better everyday life for many people."

—Ikea

"Create economic opportunity for every member of the global workforce."

—LinkedIn

"A computer on every desk and in every home."

—Microsoft

"A world without poverty."

—Oxfam

"Build the best product, cause no unnecessary harm, use business to inspire and implement solutions to the environmental crisis."

—Patagonia

"One day, all children in this nation will have the opportunity to attain an excellent education."

—Teach for America

Here are three steps to writing your vision statement:

Step 1: Write down an action verb that will make the perfect scenario happen. Action verbs are words that show a person doing something—an action—such as building, creating, developing, finding, managing, organizing, strengthening, and teaching.

Step 2: Write down one or two phrases that show the perfect scenario of your future. What is your ideal life? This could be your vision statement. But let's go a bit deeper.

Step 3: Write down who will benefit, besides you, from this perfect scenario.

Now take these steps and put them into a statement: My vision is to (step 1) (step 2) for (step 3). Here's how it looks for Marisa's vision statement:

Step 1: Action verb—To create

Step 2: Perfect scenario—A world free from labels and full of opportunity

Step 3: Who will benefit—People who want to improve themselves and others

Marisa's Vision: My vision is to create a world free from labels and full of opportunity for those who seek to improve themselves and the lives of those around them.

CHAPTER TEN REFLECTION

People treat you the way you allow them to treat you. This chapter's reflection isn't about how you want to be treated, though. It's an eye-opener about how you treat others. As a leader, do you take care of your people even if they don't expect you to? That's a powerful thought. It's the power of aligning your values with your vision.

For this reflection, consider any instances where you might walk all over someone because they let you, or maybe you show up late because you know the other person will wait for you. Take a moment to become more mindful of how you treat others, whether they allow you to or not. There's no need to take advantage of anyone. As a relatable leader, it's vital to find ways to treat people how you would like to be treated, not how they allow you to treat them.

In this chapter's reflection, we'd like you to consider the following questions:

What is the role you fill in your life?
What does *just do you* look like?
When you take away all the other titles and what those titles imply, who are you?
What do you value?

Now complete this phrase out loud or in the silence of your mind, and write it down:
My vision is to . . .

11 Plotting with Purpose

Indifference and procrastination lead to many project failures. In an article titled "How Project Managers Should Deal with Procrastination at Work," author, copywriter, and digital project management consultant Anne Meick states, "Procrastination kills personal productivity and, in turn, team productivity."[1]

Early in my career, I promised myself that when I became a project manager, I would care about my team and my projects, and I would avoid procrastination whenever possible.

Today, after twenty years and over nearly a hundred projects later, I have worked very hard to keep this promise. I've learned that a project manager above all is a relatable leader for the people they work with and for the circumstances. Being a project manager has taught me to become an organized, ethical, confident, assertive, creative, fair, and dedicated member of society. The way I interacted with my teams bled into how I interacted with my wife, parents, friends, and peers. This deepened my relationships on many levels, and by blending my project manager self with my personal self, I became not only a better leader, but a better person as well.

Keeping vigilant of Meick's warning reminds me to set an example for my team and my peers: My vision, to create a world full of relatable leaders for the betterment of society, reminds me to recognize the value of leadership at levels within a project's team and that having a team of a relatable leaders is critical to a project's success.

The companion to a vision statement is a mission statement. Whereas vision statements are high-concept, future-looking statements, mission statements are strategies for how we want to live our lives, and they guide us toward getting the results we want. Your mission statement reveals your purpose.

Scholar Imen Keskes states that "inspiration is defined as inspiring and empowering followers to enthusiastically accept and pursue challenging goals and a mission."[2] This suggests that we should have a personal mission and goals that inspire us to achieve and exceed them.

I think everyone should have a personal mission. I didn't solidify my personal mission until I considered what wasn't working in my life. Then fixing what I didn't like became my mission. Once I began to plot with purpose, my goals became value-added and the satisfaction at achieving those goals increased more than a hundredfold.

In this chapter, we're going to focus on plotting with purpose by providing

* ways to write your mission statement,
* three concepts of leadership skills,
* ways to live the leadership lifestyle, and
* a reflection upon what success looks like to you.

By using backward planning and starting with your end goal in mind, you established your vision. Not everyone will draft their vision first, but as a project manager, I find it's more efficient for me to know where I'm going (vision) before planning how to get there (mission).

Now it's time to write your mission statement, which is key to plotting your leadership development plan. The mission statement shows how you intend to achieve your vision.

SIMON'S MISSION STATEMENT

Through compassion and concern for others, I want to expand my community awareness and continue to learn all I can, so I can live a culturally agile, authentic life.

Before we dive into the three steps to writing your mission statement, let's look at some examples of mission statements:

"To be a teacher. And to be known for inspiring my students to be more than they thought they could be."

—Oprah Winfrey

"My mission in life is not merely to survive, but to thrive; and to do so with some passion, some compassion, some humor, and some style."

—Maya Angelou

"To have fun in [my] journey through life and learn from [my] mistakes."

—Richard Branson

Mission statements can be for an individual, a family, a group, or an organization, and once you get the basic formula down, they're a great way to brand who you are as a person, a member of a family, a group, or an organization. We're giving you a basic formula to draft your mission statement, but as a leader and the CEO of your life, we don't expect you to follow the formula exactly. As you can see from the examples above, there is plenty of room for revisions and to make this statement your own. Still, we feel the following three steps are the easiest starting line to get those creative juices flowing in a productive direction.

Step 1: Write down the two or three values from Three Ways to Figure Out Your Values in chapter ten.

Step 2: Write down one or two goals from your Gantt chart in chapter nine.

Step 3: Write down why you want to accomplish these goals.

Now take these steps and put them into a statement: Through (step 1), I want to (step 2), so I can (step 3).

Here's how it looks for Marisa's mission statement:

Step 1: Values—Authenticity, creativity, and optimism

Step 2: Goal—To produce meaningful and sustainable results

Step 3: Why—For the betterment of the human condition

Marisa's Mission: Through authenticity, creativity, and optimism, I want to produce meaningful and sustainable results, so I can support efforts toward the betterment of the human condition.

LEADERSHIP SKILLS

As the CEO of your life, you are the final decision maker for every aspect of your life. When you view all your actions and decisions through the lens of being a leader with the ability to influence others, you will see how having basic leadership skills will support your growth as a leader.

In chapter nine, we introduced the concept of the Gantt chart for tracking your experiences to help you become a relatable leader, and we suggested writing down at least ten experiences. If you've been keeping a Gantt chart, now's a great time to reference it. If not, you can use this time to jot down some new experiences and add more experiences as you read on.

As you're considering the experiences that will best help you cultivate your relatability, consider how leadership skills are often grouped into three categories: administrative, interpersonal, and conceptual.[3] Relatable leadership relies heavily on tapping into all three to live a leadership lifestyle, both personally and professionally. As an emerging leader, you might already excel in at least one of the three. As you read through the next section, think about experiences that will strengthen your foundation in all three categories, not just your strengths or your weaknesses.

Administrative

Administrative skills focus on the skills leaders need to be able to effectively run an organization, manage projects, and be an effective member of a team. These include managing people, managing time and resources, and showing technical competence.

Managing people is managing personalities. Over the years I've noticed that even when you have a solid plan in place, a person can stall your process. If you ask your supervisors, managers, or directors what consumes most of their time, they might say managing people, but they might also say dealing with issues. Well, those issues were created by someone, so knowing how to effectively manage people is a skill that all leaders should develop.

Families are a good place to gauge your skill level at managing people. When several family members plan a trip, they will probably each have their own ideas of how that trip should happen. Even when there is a clear leader, like a parent planning a vacation for two children, the itinerary could be flawless, but the personalities of those children would also need to be managed if the parent wanted to leave on time and stay within budget during the vacation.

As you're considering which experiences to include in your Gantt chart, perhaps one of them should be dealing with a staff issue by advising someone who's facing a problem or where you're encouraging an emerging leader to do their best. If you're looking for an experience on a smaller scale, consider offering to plan your next weekend adventure with some friends.

Managing resources is something you've probably been doing since you became an adult. Paying bills, buying groceries, and giving gifts are good examples of managing resources in your personal life. In a leadership capacity, you'll also need to know how to get resources and how to distribute them. It's pretty uncommon for leaders to be able to get everything they need for everyone on their teams or in their organization, so we encourage you to think about what kinds of experiences will give you exposure to finding, obtaining, and distributing resources on time and on budget.

When you're considering the types of experiences you might want to add to your Gantt chart to enhance your resource managing skills, consider coaching or being part of any extracurricular activity with children. You may have to negotiate, fundraise, and deal with multiple vendors to obtain your resources—all while enhancing your relatability. Volunteering for an organization that might have limited funds or chairing an event like a fundraiser or a work-related holiday party are other useful experiences.

Technical competence means that you are knowledgeable in the area that you're leading. When leaders have technical competence, they know the details of how to do the job of the people they are leading. As you expand your responsibilities or the number of departments you're leading, you may not have technical competence in all areas. You might be leading the IT department but not know how to set up a new employee's email.

As the CEO of your life, you are the expert of how to live your life, but you might not have technical competence in how to assess a performance review, for instance. In this example, the experiences you want to add to your Gantt chart would be ones where you get to measure the success of something, such as judging an essay contest or completing a self-evaluation at work.

Interpersonal

Soft skills such as interpersonal skills, including communication, conflict resolution, cultural agility, emotional intelligence, and compassion, are sometimes the hardest skills to master. In fact, in order to become a relatable leader, you must be able to focus on expanding yourself through experiences so that your authentic self, now expanded, is relatable. Developing your interpersonal skills helps you balance *just do you* with being a relatable leader. These skills involve your interaction with others, so some examples of experiences you might want to add to your Gantt chart could include team-based activities, such as sitting on a board with other leaders, volunteering to chair or organize an event, or taking point on a new initiative at work.

Being socially perceptive is keenly important for emerging leaders because, unless you are the founder, CEO, and president without a board, you are simultaneously managing two groups: your team and the executive team above you. Effectively managing your team requires creating a cohesive team of motivated individuals who can produce results for the executive team and other stakeholders. The executive team may have a direct impact on your work and your team's work, so being able to understand its ideas and how to implement them is critical. So is knowing how to effectively manage outside stakeholders needed to maintain support and how to protect your team from disruptive outside influences and politics. Having social skills is a key asset with the benefit of being able to affect change and lead others toward a common goal.

Emotional intelligence isn't a new concept, and we've mentioned it earlier in the book. If this is an area where you excel, then consider adding experiences to your Gantt chart that will enhance these skills so others can observe and learn from your expertise. If this is an area where you need more work, then add experiences that will allow you to gain more sensitivity to your own emotions and the impact your emotions and reactions have on others around you. Remember, as a leader you set the tone in a room.

The three main concepts associated with emotional intelligence are self-awareness, self-regulation, and empathy or compassion. Self-aware leaders understand their strengths and leverage them to move their teams forward. They understand and are aware of their weaknesses in order to mitigate the chances of compromising teamwork or progress. People tend to trust leaders who are self-confident yet humble. Leaders who know how to self-regulate are able to regulate their emotions and mental faculties. People tend to trust leaders who are calm in the face of adversity, treat others with respect and dignity, are trustworthy, and have consistent values.

As leaders, we have to manage interpersonal conflict. This can be stressful for some leaders whose personalities are not instinctively able to handle conflict. Since conflict is complex, we recommend leaders who want to be effective and relatable seek training that will dive deep into how to handle interpersonal conflict and conflict resolution.

Conceptual

Conceptual skills are critical in every aspect of your life. These skills include creating visions, strategic planning, and problem-solving. Leaders should have the ability to not only create a vision, but also get others excited about working toward that vision. Relatable leaders will know how to create visions that have meaning for not just themselves but for those around them. Review the vision statement you wrote in chapter ten and consider how you could get others to be a part of realizing that vision. For example, my vision is to create a world full of relatable leaders for the betterment of society. If everyone embraces the realities of being relatable leaders, I'm convinced it will benefit society as a whole. I created my vision with the idea that it will improve not just my life, but the lives of those around me and beyond as well.

In addition to knowing how to create a vision, leaders should know how to implement their visions. Earlier in this chapter you wrote a mission statement showing how you intend to achieve your vision. This is the high-level statement of your strategic plan. Strategic planning gives a framework for how a leader and their teams work toward the implementation of goals to reach a vision. As part of strategic planning, effective leaders need to be able to problem solve. This means that they need to be able to identify the problem, create some solutions, and implement the correct solution for a favorable outcome.

Vision and mission statements are not constrained to your life or one organization. In fact, any of the experiences you've used to enhance your administrative and interpersonal skills can cultivate your conceptual skills. At a basic level, every experience could offer you the opportunity to create a vision, plan, and problem solve.

LIVING THE LEADERSHIP LIFESTYLE

We can't say this enough: Having clear goals, a vision, and mission statements is critical for your leadership development. Leadership is not a trait. Leadership is a lifestyle.

When you're living your most authentic life, you're living the leadership lifestyle. After establishing where you want to go and determining a path for getting there, you'll need to investigate what you might need to change about your habits, skills, or attitude in order to make the journey successful. Change must happen for growth. Stagnancy is boring. So here's where we dig into three ways you can be amazing and make change happen.

1. Keep yourself open to possibilities.
2. Understand your strengths.
3. Surround yourself with people who support your vision of how you want to live your life.

KEEP YOURSELF OPEN TO POSSIBILITIES

During a community leadership development program session Marisa attended, one presenter challenged the participants with an improvisational activity. The presenter introduced the concept of "yes, and . . ."—the generally accepted rule in improvisation that each improviser engage with what other improvisers say and extend that line of thinking rather than shut it down. This turns our attention to the potential of the interaction and is another way to reframe how you approach your leadership journey. With a "yes, and . . ." mentality, relatable leaders focus on possibilities rather than limitations. This aligns with our first thought of *why not?*

Even though something might potentially go wrong, the word *yes* has a positive connotation for most. Still, focusing on the potential entails more than having a positive mindset. Relatable leaders understand that focusing on the potential means finding solutions rather than looking at ways something might not work. Perhaps because potential can be linked with possibility, relatable leaders see opportunities where others might be swayed by negative thoughts. After decades of working with and observing leaders in all stages of their leadership development, we've come to the conclusion that effective leaders who focus on the potential have found a way to reduce, if not remove entirely, negativity from their daily interactions.

You can't get to where you want to be if you keep letting negativity hold you back. Without all that negative stuff holding you down—it's exhausting holding on to heavy things like bitterness and anger—you'll be able to take advantage of new opportunities. When your brain isn't circling the drain of negativity, you'll be able to think of solutions to relevant issues in your life. Once we actively focus on shifting our thoughts from the roadblocks to the potential, good things happen. It starts within us, with our own self-talk, before it expands to how we express our thoughts around others. This is the power of intrapersonal communication.

Why is deleting negativity such a key factor? Leadership has an interconnected relationship with influence. If you're a leader and negativity pulls you down, you will pull down those around you as well. It's sometimes too easy to let negative thoughts infiltrate your mind, and as we noted earlier, you as the leader set the mood in any situation. If your mood is negative about yourself and the world around you, then you're not focusing on the positive ways to improve yourself and others.

Research shows how negativity impacts our health. There are health benefits of positive thinking, including increased life span, lower rates of depression, lower levels of distress, greater resistance to the common cold, better psychological and physical well-being, better cardiovascular health and reduced risk of death from cardiovascular disease, and better coping skills during hardships and times of stress.[4] Reframing the way you accept something can turn a negative thought into a positive thought. If you think there's no way something will work, consider shifting your thought to a more positive *I can try to make it work.*

Some types of negativity are easier to ignore than others. It may not happen overnight, but you can turn your back on negativity and see the positive potential in your life, cultivating a more self-accepting and optimistic outlook.

UNDERSTAND YOUR STRENGTHS

Greg Norman, golfing legend and chair and CEO of the Greg Norman Company, said, "Know your strengths. Then play to them."[5] Understanding your strengths requires more than just identifying what you're good at; it involves exploring how your strengths form your path in life. If you take a moment to list your strengths, you will see that they span many categories and contexts. You get clues about how you perceive yourself and how others perceive you, and then you can make a comparison between your perception and those of others. If you think you're a fantastic public speaker, your colleagues support this perception, and your audience gives you positive feedback, then this perception of public speaking as a strength has been triangulated and should be considered one of your greatest strengths.

TRIANGULATION

Triangulation is a method used in research to validate a claim. The credibility of a claim increases when more than one person reaches the same outcome or conclusion.

Here's an exercise to use triangulation to help you discover your strengths. Think about how you behave and react in your daily personal and professional life. How do you usually feel when waking up, during the day, and while falling asleep? What are you usually doing? Write down all the strengths you think you have. After you have your list, think about the people around you, those who are closest to you, and those you spend the most time with in your day. Ask them to tell you three strengths they think you have, then compare your list with theirs. The matches are your triangulated strengths. Now consider why others did not note the strengths on your list that were not triangulated. In what ways could you transform these untriangulated strengths into triangulated ones?

Hopefully, you'll reach the point in your leadership journey where all your strengths are triangulated by the people in your life with whom you interact the most. This means you're living authentically and holistically. It means your leadership style is your lifestyle.

Relatedly, if any of your people mentioned strengths that you didn't have on your list, here's a great moment to reflect upon why you didn't consider those strengths and maybe add them to your list.

Relatable leaders not only understand their strengths, but they also know how to identify emerging leaders and cultivate their strengths. You can use this same exercise with others to help them triangulate their lists. By understanding your strengths, you can focus on ways in which using your strengths align with your personality and potential. You can leverage your strengths to help you reach your goals. Since strengths are things you're already good at, and most likely come instinctively to you, you're already living authentically by spotlighting your strengths.

Other ways to evaluate your strengths are through formal assessments like a SWOT analysis (strengths, weaknesses, opportunities, and threats), an EQ test (emotional intelligence test), the HEXACO model (as mentioned earlier in the book), and personality tests like the Myers-Briggs and DiSC profile (dominance, influence, steadiness, and conscientiousness). The benefit to formal assessments is that they give you a range of where your weaknesses fall on a scale. Weaknesses are helpful to identify so you can find ways to work around them, but we caution you not to get stuck and allow the identification of your weaknesses to bring you down or lower your self-esteem. Everyone has weaknesses, and relatable leaders find ways to change their weaknesses into experiences that won't hold them back from achieving their goals.

SURROUND YOURSELF WITH SUPPORTIVE PEOPLE

Finding the right people to help you achieve your goals is critical for your long-term growth as a person and as a leader. It may be challenging for you to find others who have visions that align with yours. When you meet someone, you might know right away whether you could work well with them, or it might take some time to get to know a person before you can make an informed decision. You may not have a choice, such as when you're hired to be part of an already established team. But you have more flexibility in your personal life to surround yourself with supportive people.

Some of us aren't born with the natural ability to judge people accurately; however, by examining yourself and those already in your circle, you'll be able to see if you're surrounded by the type of supportive people who will help you achieve your vision. Since my vision is to create a world full of relatable leaders for the betterment of society, I need to make sure that the people on my personal team—and in my workplace whenever possible—also support the vision of creating more relatable leaders. Which is why cultivating your relatability starts with you.

As you embrace the concept that there is no box, you can make a conscious effort to seek out positive supporters who expand your normative viewpoint. The keys here are positive supporters and normative viewpoint. If you surround yourself with negative supporters, they can interfere with your commitment to focusing on the positive potential. Finding supportive people who share viewpoints different from yours will give you the opportunity to think critically about what you believe. By learning to expand your worldview, you will challenge what you've always known and learn what more there is. One way to do this is to shift your thinking from there's an inside and outside of a box to there is no box.

Why does the concept of no boxes matter? Because diversity stretches our default positions in so many ways. When we embrace the no boxes concept, we no longer see limits and boundaries stopping us from gaining opportunities to grow.

That saying about not putting all your eggs in one basket easily transfers to why you should diversify your financial investments. The diagnostic teams seeking answers to unknown diseases have better results when the doctors have different backgrounds and view the problems from different perspectives. In order to create new ideas, we're told to look at things from a different angle. So, surrounding yourself with people who both support your vision and help expand your normative viewpoint will allow you to focus on moving forward toward your goals.

In all my research and professional experience, I've yet to discover two phenomena: the literal overnight success and the leader who single-handedly achieves something universally astonishing. While these two phenomena certainly appear to be real, I believe people perceive them as happening because leaders plan for success and surround themselves with people who support them in their pursuits.

The Overnight Success

How does one become an overnight success? They plot their journey with purpose. Each decision they make contributes to an action that leads to a result that culminates in the moment when they appear to be an overnight success. Some might call it dumb luck or being in the right place at the right time. Others might suggest blood, sweat, and tears helped make it happen. Regardless of their journey, some are labeled an overnight success, but we know it took more than one night.

Everyone's idea of success is different, and you have to internalize what success means to you. Only then can you plot with purpose to get you where you want to be.

The Single-Handed Great Achievement

After you've had a moment to envision what success looks like for you, you'll want to figure out how to achieve that success, and it won't happen in a vacuum or all by yourself. In fact, I would pay good money for a conversation with the person who single-handedly achieved something considered universally astonishing. We all have support systems or lack of support systems that provide the catalyst, the motivation, or the knowledge to continue moving toward our goals. For that reason, as the CEO of your life, it's your job to build the right team to help you achieve the success you envision for yourself.

CHAPTER ELEVEN REFLECTION

Plotting with purpose means we get to intentionally make a plan (mission) that will add value to our lives and the lives of those around us. We know what we want our world to look like (vision), and gaining more experiences will help strengthen our foundation for living the leadership lifestyle. When we keep ourselves open to possibilities, we're looking at who is around us and how those people help us on our path.

In this chapter's reflection, consider what success looks like for you and how you're going to get there.

Now complete this phrase out loud or in the silence of your mind, and write it down:

My mission is to . . .

12 Own Your Life

If you took the time to read this book, then the least you can be is amazing. In an article for *Inc.*, leadership executive coach Lolly Daskal states that one of the twelve things people regret the most before they die is this: "I wish I had lived up to my full potential. Live up to your own aspirations, not down to others' expectations. There is no passion to be found in settling for a life that is less than the one you are capable of living."[1]

Hopefully this book helped expand your worldview, making you aware of how to be more relatable to other leaders and to those you lead. Through intrapersonal communication and taking ownership of your life, you can self-lead first to become a better leader for others. We are believers in self-talk, and we think using reflection and being truthful with ourselves is critical for personal growth. So now it's time to make some commitment to your own leadership development plan. Commit to your growth as a leader. There isn't just one way to get to where you want to be. The plan doesn't have to be set in concrete, but your resolve to become amazing does.

It's not about ideas. It's about making ideas happen. It's not their journey. It's yours. And we all have different starting lines. In this chapter, we're going to focus on how to own your life by providing

* guidance for what leadership means,
* an examination of leadership development plans,
* advice for preparing a personal leadership development plan,
* an analysis of an example of a leadership development plan,
* final thoughts on owning your life, and
* a reflection upon what you used to think versus what you think now.

USED TO AND NOW

We used to think *leadership* meant job creators versus job seekers, as in leaders are those who create visions and hire others to help them build their dreams. And now we think leadership is a state of being that can be found throughout any level and sphere of life, not just at the top of organizations and not just in the workplace.

One of our friends, a mid-level analyst career-wise, is a Girl Scout troop leader, a hobbyist photographer, and an emerging project manager. She makes high-level, high-risk decisions daily, and we are fortunate enough to witness her competencies in several areas outside of her day job. It would be easy to miss her ability to influence others or create a shared mission toward a common goal, but after reflecting upon what leadership means, we've been able to better see leadership skills in others.

During my doctoral journey, I focused on leadership development through the experiential learning process rather than through fixed learning traits. After interviewing alumni of community leadership development programs, I found that leaders engage at any stage in the experiential learning cycle with any given experience. I also found that the way an experience is processed is highly individualized, as is the leadership development process.

Today's leaders face complex and daunting challenges. Leaders who know how to empower their teams enhance their organizations. The rise of management education, business schools, and leadership development elicits the question of whether leadership can be taught—and learned. The importance of influencing behaviors in leadership development is apparent, and organizations are spending more time and money on leadership development, recognizing that every organization benefits from strong leadership.

The W. K. Kellogg Foundation examined fifty-five leadership development programs and found that a large portion of the programs focused on fellowship, community service, and grassroots leadership designed to solve specific community-based issues. These leadership development programs shared several common features:

* leadership without formal authority,
* development of individual competencies and organizational capacities,
* inclusivity of diverse communities, and
* broad social environments.

The researchers found that when employees were given leadership development opportunities, the result was often a positive work environment. As a result, leadership development programs benefit not just the individual, but also the organization.

Leaders continue to learn even as they continue to lead.

LEADERSHIP DEVELOPMENT PLANS

A leadership development plan is used to enhance and refine a leader's abilities. Such a plan can serve as a road map to guide a leader toward greater focus on the objectives while charting a course to navigate any challenges. Creating a leadership development plan can

* refine an emerging leader's pathway to success,
* enhance an existing leader's journey,
* serve as a road map to guide a leader toward stated objectives, and
* chart a course to navigate any challenges.

Relatable leadership is essential for the success of any organizational initiative. To become a successful relatable leader, ethics and professional conduct should take a central stage in the value-driven decision-making process of any leader. Relatable leadership incorporates characteristics of authentic, inspiring, servant, and transformational leadership theories.

To develop both an ethical awareness and leadership expertise, you want to examine your vision and mission as it relates to the leadership theories that highlight the key characteristics of relatable leadership. This is key when reflecting on the leader you are now, what kind of leader you want to be, and the experiences you may use to get there.

PREPARING YOUR PERSONAL LEADERSHIP DEVELOPMENT PLAN

In most cases, a leadership development plan guides an emerging leader in ways to become a better leader. Ideally, a leadership development plan includes steps to take in order to become a better leader. Since we all have different starting lines, everyone's plan will be, as the name suggests, personal to the individual. Everyone can focus on what would be required for their own growth and not simply follow a generic program. This assumes that the individual already has a sense of their positionality and an idea of what a leader means to them.

Throughout this book, we've been reflecting on ways relatable leaders cultivate their relatability. Self-assessing where you are now versus where you want to be will help you determine what to include in your plan. Plans are fluid, so as you develop in one area or gain insight in other areas of your leadership lifestyle, remember that your plan is open for revisions. Your initial basic plan could include seven sections:

1. Vision statement
2. Mission statement
3. Objectives
4. Approaches
5. Assumptions
6. Assistance
7. Documentation

Your vision statement is a high-concept, future-looking statement that reminds you where you want to be, and your mission statement shows how you intend to achieve your vision. Objectives are what you're seeking to accomplish. These are the goals you aim to achieve by creating a personal leadership development plan. Obviously, the main objective should be to become a better leader, but in what ways? If leadership is about influence, are you hoping to expand your reach of influence? Do you want to supervise more people at work? Would you like to change the world? This is where the objectives become personalized. Objectives should include a timeline, specific areas for improvement, and address current self-assessed weaknesses.

Approaches are the attitudes and strategies with which you're undertaking the personal leadership development journey. Do you plan to take a personality test first or maybe write out a couple of lines stating your positionality? After you've assessed your existing state, will you focus on your vision and mission or review the goals (experiences) listed on your Gantt chart from chapter nine and jump into those experiences? All of these can help you identify your starting point.

Assumptions are the basic ideas that are accepted as certain going into the plan. Just as everyone's starting line is different, so, too, are the assumptions we make as we create our plans. Do you assume you will be successful, that you will have help as you complete your plan, that your leadership development will be an ongoing endeavor, that you will be promoted at some point during the implementation of your plan, that you will be a better person and a better leader once you've completed your plan?

Assistance is the ways in which you will gather support as you complete your plan. Remember earlier how we discussed the rarity of finding a single-handed achievement? That's because we believe every successful leader has had assistance in some way along their journey. Who will be there to help you, listen to you, support you, and encourage you as you develop into the kind of leader you want to be?

Documentation is the way in which you plan to track your development. By documenting your journey, you'll have a concrete way to hold yourself accountable. We've used two visuals to help you organize your growth: the portfolios and the Gantt chart. Ideally, both of these would be used together. The portfolios help you categorize your goals so that you can see how balanced your growth is in all areas of your life. The Gantt chart is a great way to document your experiences and gives you a visual to reflect on how valuable those experiences were to your growth. Consider different ways you can document other parts of your leadership development.

EARLY VERSION OF MARISA'S PERSONAL LEADERSHIP DEVELOPMENT PLAN

This plan has since gone through many revisions as each stage was expanded upon and other details are added. Hopefully, this plan will help you draft your own.

Vision

My vision is to create a world free of labels and full of opportunity for those who seek to improve themselves and the lives of those around them.

Mission

Through authenticity, creativity, and optimism, I want to produce meaningful and sustainable results so I can support efforts toward the betterment of the human condition.

Objectives

1. To create an experiential leadership plan that will be implemented during the summer with lessons learned documented and revisions completed for future development
2. To enhance my self-assessed leadership strengths: communication and development of others
3. To expand upon the leadership competencies that appeal to my journey: innovation and entrepreneurship
4. To recognize and address my leadership blind spots and weaknesses: networking, cultural agility, compassion, and ethical practice

Approach

My approach to this personal leadership development plan is fourfold:

1. Review a previous leadership self-assessment test that breaks down my responses into five categories: model the way, inspire a shared vision, challenge the process, enable others to act, and encourage the heart.[2]
2. Create a personal mission and vision that will inspire action from myself and others at all levels in their lives, incorporating what I consider exemplary leadership practices.
3. Reflect on ways in which my leadership blind spots and weaknesses prevented me from achieving the best outcomes for my team.
4. Create ways to assess my development:
   a. Interview current (traditional, hierarchical) leaders about their own journey to leadership (how they arrived and their expectations versus realizations).
   b. Identify and create conversations with leaders lacking the traditional title to increase my own awareness of how leadership is practiced as a lifestyle and not a trait.
   c. Seek genuine feedback from my team regarding my quality of work, delegation style, communication strategies, team development, processes, and long-term plans.

Assumptions

This personal leadership development plan has five basic assumptions:

1. This plan will take place under the guidance of an experienced leader.
2. This plan will be implemented with a start and end date, and will utilize real-life experiences in the private sector to contribute to learning development.
3. This plan will involve industry professionals who encourage leadership development.

4. This plan was developed with the end goal of creating a balanced and enhanced scholar-practitioner, not simply a singular leader in the private sector.
5. This plan considers leadership as a lifestyle rather than a destination.

Assistance

Mentoring will play an enormous role in my personal leadership development plan. In order to further my own development, I will enlist the assistance of seasoned industry professionals, emerging entrepreneurs, and my own team at work for opportunities and honest feedback. This feedback will hopefully include ways I can better my own lead-by-example mantra, continue my scholarship, and be more proactive in recognizing talent to mentor along the publishing pipeline. I will reach out to former assistants of mine who now have amazing careers in publishing and seek their feedback regarding how working with me helped align their ideas and dreams with implementation, and I will utilize their feedback to assess my own leadership pathway.

Documentation

My journey will be documented through journal entries, a Gantt chart, and a final reflection paper, with a presentation and workshop developed for my team and my future emerging entrepreneur-focused clients.

BREAKING DOWN MARISA'S PERSONAL LEADERSHIP DEVELOPMENT PLAN

Given the depth and significance of leadership theories, classic and contemporary, and the abundance of literature, academic and otherwise, developing my leadership plan proved intriguing. In accepting my role as a scholar-practitioner and change agent, I addressed those difficult and uncomfortable challenges facing my organization and my industry. But first, I listened and learned, collecting knowledge to help me move forward successfully in pursuit of my goals.

This earlier personal leadership development plan took place over one summer. It had minimal adjustments in an effort to further my development and understanding of what is leadership and how my increasing awareness of myself as a leader could be leveraged to improve myself and those I work with. I've said this before, and I'll repeat it until I die: I don't have a job; I have a purpose. I work within the publishing industry, and in all my roles, my personal leadership development plan has helped me focus on the heart of my journey.

So let's break down the plan, starting with the objectives, so you can see how it relates to what I'm trying to develop and how you can craft your own plan in a similar fashion.

Plan Objectives

My role in the publishing industry had found me participating in difficult conversations relating to racial and economic inequity. Generating authentic interactions with leaders in the community is critical for the success of my mission. Therefore, when developing my personal leadership development plan, I focused on enhancing my strengths and spotlighting my weaknesses for improvement, and I created a plan with four objectives. In your plan, I suggest you start with four objectives similar to mine, and then depending on your vision, you may add more. Additionally, depending on your preferred style of planning, you might want to write out more detailed objectives than I did.

My first objective was to create an experiential leadership plan with the lessons learned documented and revisions completed for future development that I could implement during the summer. In researching how to create the best plan for my goals, I borrowed from Nick Petrie's white paper on future trends of leadership development and the idea of transferring greater developmental ownership to the individual.[3] By doing so, I accepted the role as CEO of my life rather than wait for someone else to suggest I take a leadership development workshop or class. This meant I would have the ability to focus on what would be required for my own growth rather than a generic program, with the *why* defined in the preplan and the *how* achieved as the summer progressed. It also meant that in working with my clients, I focused on the idea that they are the CEOs of their careers and would be active partners in the success of both of us.

When you're creating your first objective, consider your timeline. Summer offered me a good amount of time to work on my plan without a lot of other stuff happening like holidays and such. Three months seemed like long enough for me to dive into my plan but also short enough for me to see results.

My second objective, to enhance my self-assessed leadership strengths—communication and development of others—led to varying degrees of success. I've always considered communication and development of others a given; however, I learned the development of others does not mean creating replicas of myself. In our industry, it is critical for those I work with to know which talent (emerging writers seeking traditional publication deals through the literary agency) to sign and who to decline to represent.

We love finding raw writers and developing them into people with successful careers. But sometimes we are unable to develop those people into the leaders they need to be in order to achieve their goals. I continue to pursue this objective, with a white paper in progress on managing our expectations and drafting our vision for enabling the full potential of emerging writers.

Your second objective in your personal leadership development plan should focus on your self-assessed leadership strengths. What are your strengths as a leader? How will you expand on those strengths?

My third objective was to expand upon the leadership competencies that appeal to my journey: innovation and entrepreneurship. Understanding the impact of entrepreneurs on community engagement has become a passion of mine. Because of this, I began to view every interaction through the lens of leadership happening throughout an organization, and we are the CEOs of our lives. When building upon specific traits and concepts such as innovation and entrepreneurship, this framework works because a chain reaction of success occurs when people are empowered to explore solutions, tackle new challenges, and take risks. Shared experiences produce knowledge, a sense of community, and a feeling of being valued.

The third objective in your personal leadership development plan should focus on the leadership competencies that appeal to your journey. When I look at my vision to create a world free of labels and full of opportunities for those who seek to improve themselves and the lives of those around them, I consider innovation and entrepreneurship to be two key leadership competencies needed in pursuit of achieving that vision. What are two or three competencies that you need to enhance to realize your vision?

My fourth objective was to recognize and address my leadership blind spots and weaknesses: networking, cultural agility, compassion, and ethical practice. Throughout that summer, the key component I focused on for this objective was networking. Mistakenly, at first, I approached leadership as an outcome, where the people I worked with, in my collective, could interact and leverage their social networks. In the process, I discovered that leadership is a lifestyle, not an end result, and then I noticed that the team aligned more closely toward their goals and the goals of the organization. Through this changing mindset, I was able to increase my capacity by utilizing the strengths of those around me.

When you're drafting your fourth objective, consider your leadership blind spots and weaknesses. Identifying your blind spots is not an easy ask. How are you supposed to see something you can't see? I used three methods to narrow down this objective. One was to observe those I considered leaders and identify their blind spots and weaknesses. The second method was to reflect on my own leadership deficiencies. The third method was to ask those around me what they considered to be my blind spots and weaknesses. By matching your self-assessed weaknesses with what others consider to be your weaknesses, you are able to narrow down your list for this objective.

Plan Approach

My approach to my personal leadership development plan was four-fold, and after reviewing a previous leadership self-assessment I'd taken that broke down my responses into five categories (model the way, inspire a shared vision, challenge the process, enable others to act, and encourage the heart), I crafted personal vision and mission statements meant to inspire action from myself and others at all levels of their lives, incorporating what I consider exemplary leadership practices.

Another piece I wanted to develop was reflecting on ways in which my leadership blind spots and weaknesses prevented me from achieving the best outcomes for the people I work with. It is quite humbling to admit, but through journaling and deep discussions with other leaders, I discovered that overcoming my introverted tendencies in order to make polite conversation at the beginning of any interaction drained me and filled me with a sense of purposelessness. I already knew this about myself, but through this piece of the development, I realized why. Previous to this reflection, I viewed small talk as a waste of time before tackling the real reason for meeting with someone. However, I have since discovered that in order to build lasting relationships beyond the one transaction, and to incorporate new people within my circle, it is imperative that I—and they—first form a baseline for figuring out if we believe in the same set of values, and if not, what other common ground could we share. I believe this tiny adjustment to how I view small talk has increased my cultural agility in a way I might not have come to on my own. By employing compassionate communication in every interaction, I'm better able to objectively assess situations and make decisions.

This helped support me in the final approach I had originally devised: create ways to assess my development by 1) interviewing current (traditional, hierarchical) leaders about their own journeys to leadership (how they arrived and their expectations versus realizations); 2) identifying and creating conversations with leaders lacking the traditional title to increase my own awareness of how leadership is practiced as a lifestyle and not a trait; and 3) seeking genuine feedback from my team regarding my quality of work, delegation style, communication strategies, team development, processes, and long-term plans.

Plan Assumptions

The assumptions remained valid throughout the summer. One surprising twist was the level of investment I received from others encouraging me in my leadership development. Nicole Resciniti, the president of my company, encouraged me in ways I had never considered, and through this mentoring and support, I noticed an increased level of confidence in myself by the end of the summer. This also showed me the power of mentorship and ways I could initiate conversations with emerging leaders to help them along their journey.

Plan Assistance

I underestimated the value of having a mentor in my corner when I first started this journey. I thought creating experiences would be the best teacher, but having mentors who could help me unpack those experiences expanded my knowledge tenfold. Having someone provide advice and support my decisions increased my self-confidence and self-esteem. As I was developing my team and taking on my own clients, I intentionally sought honest feedback for how I could enhance my own lead-by-example mantra, continue my scholarship, and be more proactive in recognizing talent to mentor along the publishing pipeline. Surprisingly, everyone I reached out to was willing to assist me, and that says a lot about how I've succeeded in surrounding myself with supportive people.

Plan Documentation

I documented my summer's leadership development journey through journal entries and a Gantt chart, and I recommend this for everyone. Not only was the journal a great way for me to capture my immediate impressions in real time, but it allowed me to review the progress I had made months later and see the growth I'd made over several months. The Gantt chart gave me a visual to check off my goals as they happened and to make adjustments to my timeline as the summer progressed if I was missing an experience.

SAMPLE FROM MARISA'S LEADERSHIP DEVELOPMENT JOURNAL

Met with Nicole [Resciniti] today. She's perhaps the most culturally agile leader I've encountered to date. After a brief interview, which she allowed me to video, we discussed pathways for how I can help my clients reach their goals. Despite my clients all coming from a variety of backgrounds with varying levels of experience, Nicole easily slipped into their frame of reference to give me some really great advice. She also shared with me the different perspectives other industry professionals might have given certain situations I faced, and her knowing how to relate to each circumstance based on the individuals involved was nothing short of remarkable. It's that relatability that I'm developing now, and I'm convinced it's her ability to tap into her compassionate side that allows her to see a situation with 360-degree clarity.

As this journal entry shows, one benefit of documenting your interactions is to give you time to reflect on what you're processing as you grow and develop your own ideas about leaders and leadership. The time you take for reflection is critical for your growth. By reflecting—and documenting—you're confirming that the interaction you had with that leader or the time you've spent on an experience is a valuable use of your time.

This plan is old now, but at the time, I wasn't just focused on talking with leaders and creating new experiences for myself. I was keen on observing the ways in which spending time with them and on experiences could make me a better person. Since I consider time my most valuable asset, this gift of time I gave myself to explore my interactions also improved the ways in which I prioritized my life moving forward.

REFLECTING ON THIS PERSONAL LEADERSHIP DEVELOPMENT PLAN

We shouldn't compare our life with others' lives but rather compare how we are living our life with how we want to be living. The leadership development plan identifies an existing state, a proposed vision, and a timeline to accomplish the vision. Having a dedicated timeline for initiating this personal leadership development plan focused my attention on the priorities in the plan. Though some feedback was difficult to hear, such as when someone I respect said that my life "needs more balance," this helped me figure out an important piece about both of us: neither one of us has balance in our lives, and that's why it was noticeable in mine. We laughed about this, and together we decided to focus on living a balanced lifestyle.

This personal leadership development plan also contributed to an area of interest: understanding how leadership and creating engaged communities are connected, and I'm hopeful that those around me will continue to build bridges through books and scholarship in areas that mean something to us.

FINAL THOUGHTS ON OWNING YOUR LIFE

Over the years we've written down our thoughts and observations; scribbled in notebooks the advice we collected from those who came before us; and prepared, plotted, and executed numerous plans in pursuit of our growth. We took time to visualize our ideal lives, and then we narrowed it down to visualize the ideal versions of ourselves. Without labels or titles. We wrote down what images of ourselves came to mind, and we asked ourselves, do we like who we are? Are we compassionate? Are we relatable? Are we healthy?

We prefer to earn what we want in this life. We'll compete with the rest of humanity to achieve our goals, even on an uneven playing field. Let us prove whether we deserve it. We're not afraid to fail. We're afraid of being unworthy. But once we get there, we'll work to level that playing field for others who may follow.

As we deepened the conversation with ourselves and with others, we discovered they noticed our calm, our joy, and our optimism, but what we think they really saw was the sense of peace in our hearts. It's much easier to live your life when you like yourself.

We used to be two people who didn't believe they could do it. Until we did it. So, please, please remember: we all have different starting lines, and we are all the CEOs of our own lives.

Once upon a time, we decided
to follow our own advice.
Simon and Marisa Cleveland

FINAL REFLECTION

The steps to becoming relatable is a holistic approach to your lifestyle, and it starts with asking *why not*. As we said in the beginning, this book is for leaders who want an honest glimpse into how to change their worldview.

For your final reflection, we'd like you to complete this phrase out loud or in the silence of your mind, and write it down:

I used to think . . .

And now I think . . .

As you close this book, we hope you take time to celebrate the milestones along your journey to cultivating your relatability. We'd love to continue this conversation and hear your success stories.

ACKNOWLEDGMENTS

First, thank you to all the leaders who take the time to read our words. We completely appreciate those who made space for us at their table, and we cherish those who willingly join us at ours. We will never be able to acknowledge all those who helped shape our worldview leading to this book, but we do want to take the time to acknowledge those who impacted how this book was shaped.

Nicole Resciniti, everlasting thank yous and hugs for believing in us and championing this manuscript. Standing ovations to the entire team at Matt Holt and BenBella Books! Matt Holt, profound thanks for finding value in the concept that there is no box and for your expert advice and guidance as we entered this space. Katie Dickman, undying gratitude for the amazing developmental edits. You somehow managed to figure out what we meant to say and wrangled our words into a cohesive narrative. Ruth Strother, endless thanks for your flawless copy edits and little comments of encouragement throughout the manuscript. This book would not be in the shape it's in today without your careful hand. Brigid Pearson, a hundred thank yous for making it so difficult for us to choose only one cover for this book. Your creativity and all of your designs captured us completely. Mallory Hyde, big thanks for sharing your expert advice as we navigate through the marketing aspects of this process.

ACKNOWLEDGMENTS

Our acknowledgments would not be complete without thanking all the people in our lives who either taught us how to lead or allowed us to lead them. Without you, we would not have been inspired to study leadership and write this book. We are the culmination of our experiences, and those experiences wouldn't be as profoundly impactful without our families, friends, and colleagues who have shared in our nearly thirty-year journey.

NOTES

CHAPTER 2

1. Simon Cleveland and Marisa Cleveland, "Toward Cybersecurity Leadership Framework," *MWAIS 2018 Proceedings*, 2018, http://aisel.aisnet.org/mwais2018/49.
2. Cleveland and Cleveland, "Toward Cybersecurity."
3. Matt Gavin, "Authentic Leadership: What It Is & Why It's Important," *Harvard Business School Online* (blog), December 10, 2019, online.hbs.edu/blog/post/authentic-leadership.
4. Cleveland and Cleveland, "Toward Cybersecurity."
5. Cleveland and Cleveland, "Toward Cybersecurity."

CHAPTER 3

1. "Navigating Complexity," *PMI's Pulse of the Profession In-Depth Report*, September 2013, pmi.org/-/media/pmi/documents/public/pdf/learning/thought-leadership/pulse/navigating-complexity.pdf.
2. Dan Lovallo and Daniel Kahneman, "Delusions of Success: How Optimism Undermines Executives' Decisions," *Harvard Business Review*, July 2003, hbr.org/2003/07/delusions-of-success-how-optimism-undermines-executives-decisions.
3. Daniel Goleman, Richard Boyatzis, and Annie McKee, *Primal Leadership: Realizing the Importance of Emotional Intelligence* (Boston: Harvard Business School Press, 2002).

4. Graham M. Winch, "Managing Project Stakeholders," *The Wiley Guide to Project, Program, and Portfolio Management*, September 17, 2004, doi.org/10.1002/9780470172391.ch14.

5. Winch, "Managing Project Stakeholders," doi.org/10.1002/9780470172391.ch14.

6. Deborah Ancona, Thomas W. Malone, Wanda J. Orlikowski, and Peter M. Senge, "In Praise of the Incomplete Leader," *Harvard Business Review*, February 2007, hbr.org/2007/02/in-praise-of-the-incomplete-leader.

7. Nathan Bennett and G. James Lemoine, "What a Difference a Word Makes: Understanding Threats to Performance in A VUCA World," *Business Horizons* 57 (2014): 311–317.

CHAPTER 4

1. Julie Ray, "Americans' Stress, Worry and Anger Intensified in 2018," Gallup, April 25, 2019, news.gallup.com/poll/249098/americans-stress-worry-anger-intensified-2018.aspx.

2. "Stress in America 2020," American Psychological Association, accessed May 23, 2021, www.apa.org/news/press/releases/stress/2020/report-october.

3. Peter Senge, Hal Hamilton, and John Kania, "The Dawn of System Leadership," *Stanford Social Innovation Review* (Winter 2015): 10, doi.org/10.48558/yte7-xt62.

4. Joseph E. Aoun, "Commencement 2019: Reinvent Yourself so That You Can Reinvent the World," *Northeastern University*, May 3, 2019, president.northeastern.edu/2019/05/03/commencement-2019-reinvent-yourself-so-that-you-can-reinvent-the-world/.

5. David Kolb, *Experiential Learning: Experience as the Source of Learning and Development* (Englewood Cliffs, NJ: Prentice Hall, 1984), 27.

CHAPTER 5

1. Darren L. Linvill and Andrew S. Pyle, "Inquiry-based Civil Discourse Education," *Communication Teacher* 31, no. 4 (August 4, 2017): 214–219, doi.org/10.1080/17404622.2017.1358382.

2. Libby V. Morris, "Collective Action for Civil Discourse," *Innovative Higher Education* 41, no. 5 (November 2016): 361–363, doi.org/10.1007/s10755-016-9376-5.

3. Kyle Lundby and Paula Caligiuri, "Leveraging Organizational Climate to Understand Cultural Agility and Foster Effective Global Leadership," *People & Strategy* 36, no. 3 (2013): 27.

4. Christian Troster, Ajay Mehra, and Daan van Knippenberg, "Structuring for Team Success: The Interactive Effects of Network Structure and Cultural Diversity on Team Potency and Performance," *Organizational Behavior and Human Decision Processes* 124, no. 2 (2014): 245–255, doi.org/10.1016/j.obhdp.2014.04.003.

5. Donna Rich Kaplowitz, Jasmine A. Lee, and Sheri L. Seyka, "Looking to Near Peers to Guide Student Discussions About Race: To Engage High School Students in Learning About Racial Identity and Difference, Ask College Students to Lead the Discussion," *Phi Delta Kappan* 99, no. 5 (February 2018): 53, doi.org/10.1177/0031721718754814.

6. Linvill and Pyle, "Inquiry-based civil discourse education."

7. Caty Borum Chattoo, Patricia Aufderheide, Michele Alexander, and Chandler Green, "American Realities on Public Television: Analysis of the Independent Television Service's Documentaries, 2007–2016," *International Journal of Communication* 12 (2018): 1562, https://ijoc.org/index.php/ijoc/article/view/7826.

8. Neha Vora, "Free Speech and Civil Discourse: Producing Expats, Locals, and Migrants in the UAE English-Language Blogosphere," *Journal of Royal Anthropological Institute* 18, no. 4 (2012): 788, https://www.jstor.org/stable/23321450.

9. Vora, "Free speech and civil discourse," 803.

10. Kent A. Ono and Ronald L. Jackson II, "Civil Discourse in the Face of Complex Social Issues," *Critical Studies in Media Communication* 28, no. 1 (2011): 1–7, doi.org/10.1080/15295036.2010.545045.

11. Robert R. Alford and Harry M. Scoble, "Community Leadership, Education, and Political Behavior," *American Sociological Association* 33, no. 2 (April 1968): 259–272, doi.org/10.2307/2092392.

12. Elad Yom-Tov, Susan Dumais, and Qi Guo, "Promoting Civil Discourse Through Search Engine Diversity," *Social Science Computer Review* 32, no. 2 (2014): 145–154, doi.org/10.1177/0894439313506838.

13. Maria Morukian, "Expansion: The Missing Link to Sustainable Diversity and Inclusion," *Forbes*, May 4, 2020, www.forbes.com/sites/ellevate/2020/05/04/expansion-the-missing-link-to-sustainable-diversity-and-inclusion/?sh=188b6a701985.

CHAPTER 6

1. Malcolm Gladwell, *Outlier: The Story of Success* (New York: Little, Brown and Company, 2008), 184.

2. Gladwell, *Outlier*, 194.

3. Simon Sinek, "First Why and Then Trust," YouTube video, 0:48, posted by "TEDx-Maastricht," April 6, 2011, www.youtube.com/watch?v=4VdO7LuoBzM&t=.

4. Alex "Sandy" Pentland, "The New Science of Building Great Teams," *Harvard Business Review*, April 2012, https://hbr.org/2012/04/the-new-science-of -building-great-teams.

5. Manuel Velasquez, Claire Andre, Thomas Shanks, S. J., and Michael J. Meyer, "What is Ethics?," *Markkula Center for Applied Ethics*, accessed May 23, 2021, www.scu.edu/ethics/ethics-resources/ethical-decision-making/what-is -ethics/.

6. Susan Krauss Whitbourne, "We All Need Role Models to Motivate and Inspire Us," Pyschology Today, November 19, 2013, www.psychologytoday.com /us/blog/fulfillment-any-age/201311/we-all-need-role-models-motivate-and -inspire-us.

7. Evan Andrews, "8 Reasons It Wasn't Easy Being Spartan," History, September 1, 2018, www.history.com/news/8-reasons-it-wasnt-easy-being-spartan.

8. Christine Hauser, "Everyone Has a Theory About Shopping Carts," *New York Times*, June 8, 2021, www.nytimes.com/2021/06/08/style/shopping-cart-parking -lot.html.

9. Sacha Pfeiffer, "Controversial Former Beth Israel CEO Writes About Lessons Learned the Hard Way," WBUR News, February 17, 2012, www.wbur.org/news /2012/02/17/paul-levy-book.

10. John Commins, "Levy's Cautionary Tale: Don't Call for Transparency When Your Windows Are Dirty," healthleaders, May 10, 2010, www.healthleadersmedia .com/strategy/levys-cautionary-tale-dont-call-transparency-when-your -windows-are-dirty.

CHAPTER 7

1. Haim Ginott, accessed on May 23, 2021, www.haimginott.com/.

2. Tony A. Gaskins Jr., *The Dream Chaser: If You Don't Build Your Dream, Someone Will Hire You to Help Build Theirs* (Hoboken: John Wiley & Sons, Inc., 2017).

3. Elisa Houot (literary agent) in discussion with the authors, October 2021.

4. Elisa Houot.

5. Altony Lee III, email message to authors, October 6, 2021.

6. John Meyer (Hodges University President) in discussion with the authors, March 2021.

7. Ram Dass, "Promises and Pitfalls of the Spiritual Path," The Library, 1988, accessed May 23, 2021, www.organism.earth/library/document/promises-and -pitfalls.

CHAPTER 8

1. Joe Raelin, "From Leadership-as-Practice to Leaderful Practice," *Leadership* 7, no. 2 (2011): 200, doi.org/10.1177/1742715010394808.
2. Amanda Beights, email message to authors, October 5, 2021.
3. Hyoung-Yong Kim, "Effects of Social Capital on Collective Action for Community Development," *Social Behavior and Personality: An International Journal* 46, no. 6, (June 2018): 1101, doi.org/10.2224/sbp.7082.
4. Hyoung-Yong Kim, "Effects of Social Capital," 1025.
5. Scott Wituk, Sarah Ealey, Mary Jo Clark, and Pat Heiny, "Community Development Through Community Leadership Programs: Insights from a Statewide Community Leadership Initiative," *Community Development* 36, no. 2 (June 2005): 89–101, doi.org/10.1080/15575330509490177.
6. Wilson Majee, Scott Long, and Deena Smith, "Engaging the Underserved in Community Leadership Development: Step Up to Leadership Graduates in Northwest Missouri Tell Their Stories," *Community Development* 43, no. 1 (February 2012): 80–94, doi.org/10.1080/15575330.2011.645049.
7. Cecila Ayon and Cheryl Lee, "Building Strong Communities: An Evaluation of a Neighborhood Leadership Program in a Diverse Urban Area," *Journal of Community Psychology* 37, no. 8 (October 20, 2009): 975–986, doi.org/10.1002/jcop.20343.
8. Gloria Padilla, email message to authors, October 18, 2021.
9. Amanda Beights, email message to authors, October 5, 2021.
10. Amanda Beights.
11. Tarek Azzam and Ronald E. Riggio, "Community Based Civic Leadership Programs: A Descriptive Investigation," *Journal of Leadership and Organizational Studies* 10, no. 1 (February 1, 2003): 55–67, doi.org/10.1177/107179190301000105.
12. Erin O'Brien, "Foam Recycling Now Available to Collier County Residents," *NBC-2*, October 1, 2020, https://nbc-2.com/news/environment/2020/09/30/foam-recycling-now-available-to-collier-county-residents
13. John Morelli, "Environmental Sustainability: A Definition for Environmental Professionals," *Journal of Environmental Sustainability* 1, no. 1 (2011): 2–11, DOI: 10.14448/jes.01.0002.
14. Morelli, "Environmental Sustainability," 5.
15. Alexandra Spiliakos, "Tragedy of the Commons: What It Is and 5 Examples," *Harvard Business School Online* (blog), February 6, 2019, online.hbs.edu/blog/post/tragedy-of-the-commons-impact-on-sustainability-issues.

CHAPTER 9

1. Steven M.R. Covey, *The Speed of Trust: The One Thing That Changes Everything* (New York: Simon & Schuster, 2006), 241, iBook.
2. Jeffrey Pinto and Dennis Slevin, "Critical Success Factors Across the Project Life Cycle," *Project Management Journal* 19, no. 3 (June 1988): 67–75, https://www.pmi.org/learning/library/critical-success-factors-project-life-cycle-2131.
3. Pinto and Slevin, "Critical success factors."

CHAPTER 10

1. Meghan Casserly, "Atlas Shrugged: Ten Lessons from Dagny Taggart," *Forbes*, April 15, 2011, www.forbes.com/sites/meghancasserly/2011/04/15/atlas-shrugged-ten-lessons-from-dagny-taggart/?sh=7b2e27d31c9a.
2. Stedman Graham, *Identity Leadership* (New York: Hachette Book Group), 28.
3. "Values," Merriam-Webster, accessed on May 23, 2021, www.merriam-webster.com/dictionary/value.
4. Russ Harris, *The Confidence Gap: A Guide to Overcoming Fear and Self-Doubt* (Boston: Trumpeter, 2011), 208, iBook.
5. Kibeom Lee and Michael C. Ashton, The Hexaco Personality Inventory Home Page, hexaco.org/.
6. Chris Musselwhite and Tammie Plouffe, "What's Your Influencing Style?" *Harvard Business Review*, January 13, 2012, hbr.org/2012/01/whats-your-influencing-style.

CHAPTER 11

1. Anne Meick, "How Project Managers Should Deal with Procrastination at Work," *PM: The Ultimate Reference for Project Managers*, February 22, 2022, project-management.com/project-managers-dealing-with-procrastination/.
2. Imen Keskes, "Relationship Between Leadership Styles and Dimensions of Employee Organizational Commitment: A Critical Review and Discussion of Future Directions," *Intangible Capital* 10, 1 (2014): 26–51, dx.doi.org/10.3926/ic.476.
3. Peter G. Northouse, *Introduction to Leadership: Concepts and Practice* (Thousand Oaks, California: Sage Publications, 2019).
4. Mayo Clinic Staff, "Positive Thinking: Stop Negative Self-talk to Reduce Stress," Mayo Clinic, January 21, 2020, www.mayoclinic.org/healthy-lifestyle/stress-management/in-depth/positive-thinking/art-20043950.

5. Ryan Osborne, "What You Can Learn from Greg Norman," *Golf Club Style*, February 5, 2021, golfclubstyle.com/what-you-can-learn-from-greg-norman-3/.

CHAPTER 12

1. Lolly Daskal, "12 Things People Regret the Most Before They Die," *Inc.*, August 15, 2015, www.inc.com/lolly-daskal/12-things-people-regret-the-most-before-they-die.html.
2. James M. Kouzes and Barry Z. Posner, *The Leadership Challenge: How to Make Extraordinary Things Happen in Organizations* (Hoboken: John Wiley & Sons, Inc., 2012).
3. Nick Petrie, "Future Trends in Leadership Development" (White paper), Center for Creative Leadership (2014).

INDEX

ABOUT THE AUTHORS

Marisa Cleveland, EdD

Photo by Simon Cleveland

With more than two decades in the education and publishing industries, Marisa Cleveland is adamant about supporting efforts toward the betterment of the human condition. Toward that goal, she has led writing programs, chaired events and fundraisers, and mentored emerging bestselling authors and literary agents. Previous to entering the publishing industry, she gained experience in higher education administration, secondary education, and writing, including technical, grant, research, and dissertation analysis. She has been featured at various book festivals and has participated on panels and in workshops focusing on diversity, civil discourse, communications, and the state of the publishing industry. She has peer-reviewed academic publications and published fiction novels. *Gulfshore Business* and *D'Latinos* magazines honored Marisa with the 2015 Arts and Culture Face Award, and in 2014, *Gulfshore Business* selected her as a 40 Under 40 honoree. Marisa earned her Doctor of Education in Organizational Leadership from Northeastern University, her Master of

Arts in Educational Administration from George Mason University, her Master of Arts in English from National University, and her Bachelor of Arts in Speech Communications from George Mason University. She is a 2015 Leadership Marco graduate and a 2022 Leadership Collier graduate.

Simon Cleveland, PhD, EdD

Photo by Jonathan Henry

Simon Cleveland is a scholar-practitioner and lecturer at Drexel University, Georgetown University, the Johns Hopkins University, Northeastern University, Purdue University Global, and Wake Forest University. Simon holds a Doctor of Education in Organizational Leadership from Northeastern University. While earning his PhD in Information Systems from Nova Southeastern University, he was honored as the three-time recipient of the prestigious Dr. Harold Kerzner Scholarship awarded by the Project Management Institute Educational Foundation. Simon was honored with the Tropaia Award: Outstanding Faculty for his work with the Master of Professional Studies in Project Management at Georgetown University and was honored with the Excellence in Teaching Award from Zanvyl Krieger School of Arts and Sciences at the Johns Hopkins University.

He sits on four editorial review boards and is an associate editor for the *International Journal of Information Technology Project Management*, the *International Journal of Project Management and Productivity Assessment*, the *International Journal of Information and Communication Technology Education*, and the *International Journal of Smart Education and Urban Society*.

Simon has over two decades of experience in managing complex technological projects, including software systems projects for Accenture, AOL, Avanade (joint venture of Microsoft and Accenture), Department of Education, Department of Homeland Security, General Dynamics, MD Anderson Cancer Center, and NASA.

Simon is a professionally certified (PMP, CSM, CSPO, ITIL, Six Sigma Black Belt) technology expert and a dynamic researcher with over fifty peer-reviewed journal and conference publications in the fields of project management, leadership, information systems, computer mediated communication, and community engagement. Simon holds certificates in education and big data from Harvard University and Massachusetts Institute of Technology.